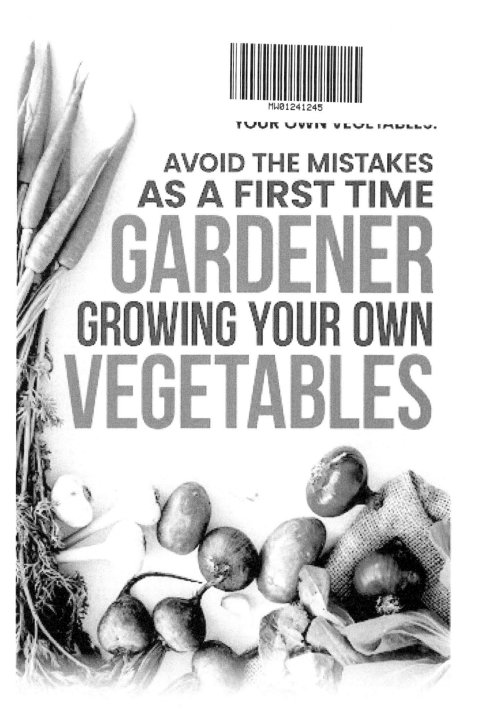

YOUR OWN VEGETABLES.

# AVOID THE MISTAKES
# AS A FIRST TIME
# GARDENER
# GROWING YOUR OWN
# VEGETABLES

## NOOR FATIMA

# AVOID THE MISTAKES AS A FIRST TIME GARDENER GROWING YOUR OWN VEGETABLES

BEGINNERS GUIDE TO PLANTING, MAINTAINING, AND HARVESTING YOUR OWN VEGETABLES.

NOOR FATIMA

# CONTENTS

*Introduction*                                                    11

1. Getting Your Garden Started                                   17
2. The Essentials of Compost                                     33
3. Your Garden Design: From Grow Bags to
   Raised Beds                                                   45
4. The Brassicas Family                                          59
5. The Leafy Greens                                              79
6. The Legumes                                                   95
7. The Nightshades                                              109
8. Digging Down For Those Root
   Vegetables                                                   121
9. Taking Advantage of the Vine Family                          137
10. How Will Herbs Help Your Vegetable
    Garden                                                      149
11. Why Your Vegetables Need Flowers                            165
12. Bringing it All Together With Companion
    Planting                                                    179
13. Get the Most Out of Your Garden Crops
    for Year-Round Self-Sustainability                          191

*Tie It All Together With a Bow*                                203
*Reference Sheet*                                               209

*"Growing your own food is like printing your own money."*

— BY RON FINLEY

# Just for You

## A free Gift for our Readers

The Green Thumb's Guide: Naturally
Controlling Garden Pests

# INTRODUCTION

Watching my uncles and aunts at their farm in Pakistan was always intriguing to me as a child. At first, it was probably the idea of them sticking their hands in fresh, soft soil. But once I started visiting them in the countryside, I was quickly enthralled by the methods they used to harvest fresh produce. As an adult, realizing that these methods can save up to $600 of food waste per year, I discovered there were many reasons to love gardening.

Like you, I want to be able to spend money on organic vegetables without breaking the bank. In fact, Whole Foods can be twice as expensive as other grocery stores per product purchase. But trusting other grocery stores in terms of where your food comes from is also unsettling. What's not upsetting is the rewarding feeling you get when providing the vegetables yourself!

Starting a vegetable garden is becoming increasingly popular with the trendy idea of "grow your own food." On the flip side, it can also be understandably overwhelming and require some serious patience. But when you start with just a small section and work 1 percent more each day on it, the snowball effect comes into play, and before you know it, you have full plump tomatoes and eye-watering onions. It's also important to understand that going too fast can cause tears, not from beautiful onions but from the lack of veggie growth.

Gardening is therapeutic and can be relaxing for everyone. Sometimes you may feel like there is really no space, but more recently, vertical gardens have become popular, providing a great decorative and functional addition to one's space. A small plot garden can also be a great option and incredibly resourceful if you prepare it well.

Another myth is that time, and lack of gardening "knowledge" could stop you from reaping the benefits. You don't need expertise because this book gives you all the tips and tricks you need to garden as productively and efficiently as possible.

What is surprising to almost everyone is that gardening is much more than planting seeds and feeding your family. There is much more of a realization that the whole process is essential. Even for me, the gardening journey goes south from time to time, and I must implement these very practices from this book to know where I went wrong. What makes me feel better is remembering what my guru gardening father would share about his mishaps with me and what he would do in times of a gardening crisis. WWDD (What Would Dad Do)?

He would breathe. Look up to the sky. And then recognize that every gardening mistake was just another excuse to spend more time playing in the dirt.

Why does this matter? Because kids don't have to worry about anything except playing around with a carefree attitude. Gardening allows us to be kids and get our hands dirty. Gardening with the right mindset can do that for you, too. And this is why it's so much more than growing vegetables. It's about finding your reason why.

While you are looking for why, let's talk about some of the incredible benefits you'll get from reading this book. Gardening is an art, but the best part is being able to follow some straightforward steps while you develop your green thumb. This book shares everything from not letting the soil be your frenemy to understanding how my veggies got so edgy.

Planting your favorites like tomatoes, radishes, onions, and more is a must in this book. But just like my nana would say, "The devil is in the detail." You will begin to understand just how far certain vegetables need to be from each other. Or, if you want to get experimental cross-pollination between certain veggies, you can create killer combinations and something interesting for the kids to look at. Have you ever seen brale? Broccoli kale combos will be the rage in 2023.

It's really no surprise that it becomes even more fun when things start to feel like a science lab. Jamie Oliver's wife, at one point, accused him of having an affair. The real deal? He was always at his vegetable garden, likely checking on his brale.

When I want to keep things more straightforward, I go back to the basics I've mastered and now want to share them with you. I was also unsure of where to start; I was somewhat interested but thought it might be just another hobby I picked up and put down.

But after having some fun along the way and really mastering the art of having a vegetable garden in all kinds of spaces, both big and small, I am forever grateful for the financial benefits, the physical benefits, and the mental health release I get from just sticking my hands in the dirt.

I'll never forget my first onion tears, but I will also remember some of the tears that were shed before ever getting a picture-perfect vegetable garden. In an effort to save you some pain, these easy-to-go-to tips and tricks will set you on the fast path to skipping Whole Foods trips altogether.

Thanks to the inspiration of my garden guru Dad, aunts, and uncles, our vegetable gardening secrets are now yours!

# 1

# GETTING YOUR GARDEN STARTED

I magine it's a beautiful sunny day, and you come out to your vegetable garden to see tomatoes, carrots, and all your favorite veggies in full bloom. There is no feeling more satisfying than reaping the reward of hard work that came straight from your fingertips. Often in the absolute beginning stages, this is all we can think about: "The finished product." But forgetting that gardening is a process rather than an end result is what causes most of us to think we are black thumbed. That's because we haven't learned "The Six P's."

*Proper Planning and Preparation Prevents Poor Planning.*

With this in mind and a little patience, we can have that beautiful sunny day with plenty of vegetables for you and your neighbors! This opening chapter is one of the most important ones! Before diving into what vegetables you want to plant, you must first understand the tools and terminology used throughout this book. The better understanding you have of the basics, the easier it will be to correct mistakes. Believe me, no matter how great of a gardener someone is, there is always a new problem to solve! Having a foundation will help you solve these bumps in the road much more quickly.

So, before planting anything, let's look at the tools you will need and the terminology. Then we can talk about soil conditions and how to work with them so you can start off on the right foot.

## TOOLS YOU'LL NEED

Starting a garden doesn't need to be a complicated process. While you will add tools as your garden grows, it's better to use the essentials than start with a shed that looks like an operating room. In other words, focusing on the essentials is better than throwing the whole kitchen sink at you!

Here are the top three items you can start with:

**1. A Shovel**

You may oddly feel overwhelmed when heading to the store to buy a shovel. While it is a simple concept, there is quite a variety to choose from. What you need is an *angled shovel*. An angled shovel will likely have a wood or a sturdy base with an arrow or triangular metalhead. Something plastic and cheap is likely to break, so investing in something sturdy is worth it long-term.

**2. Pruning Shears**

Pruning shears will be the reason you develop such a firm grip! This tool is necessary because it will help you cut back plants that need trimming as well as help you cut your fresh produce. They look similar to scissors or clippers. Something important to keep in mind for this tool is to make sure you invest in a strong pair. The blades need to be able to cut through plant stems, and they should give you a comfortable and good grip.

**3. Watering Can or Hose**

If you have a hose connected to your home, then this step is already complete! If not, you can always buy a watering can or pot. Keeping your vegetable garden hydrated but not overwatered is one of the key elements to having a green thumb.

*Tip: If your garden is planted straight in the ground, investing in a watering hose and sprayer attachment is not a bad idea.*

### Other Handy Tools for Those With an Extra Budget

While those certainly are the only tools you need to get started, there are a few other tools worth knowing about or having by your side.

### Gardening Gloves

While I like to put my hands right in the soil, not everyone feels the same way. The feeling of being so hands-on is gratifying. A pair of gardening gloves keep dirt from getting underneath your nails and can be a cute accessory if you care to dress it up!

### Kneeling Pad

A kneeling pad can be a nice cushion you put down to save your knees from feeling achy after a while. Some gardeners also like to use stools at different points. This only works for certain parts of the process as you'll need to get close to the soil for much of the time.

**Hand Trowel**

Having an angled shovel can handle all the gardening jobs but sometimes, having a hand shovel makes things easier. It can be a good substitute for specific situations.

## THE GREEN THUMB TERMINOLOGY

The Green Thumb Terminology found here can be used as a reference page. I found that when showing my neighbors how to garden, our conversations would get lost in translation. Finally, after a decade, I realized just how important understanding the terminology is.

Here is a quick bullet list of the most important terms. Don't stress about memorizing them all right off the bat. You can come back to this page when applicable.

- **Annuals** - A plant that goes through an entire life cycle in one year. They germinate, flower, set seeds, and die. This allows for a short-term commitment.
- **Biennials** - Instead of one year to complete a life cycle, these plants take two years to go through the same process as an annual.
- **Perennials** - These plants last a long time and will likely bloom once (sometimes more) a year and many years afterward.

- **Dormancy** - This is the way plants survive the winter. It is their hibernation state. It may look like nothing is happening on the surface but underneath, plants are conserving energy to survive the climate.
- **Companion planting** - Some plants grow better together. The process of growing one or more plants next to each other for the benefit of one or both is companion planting.
- **Compost** - A mixture of decayed vegetables and plants that can be put back into the soil to help plants grow and refresh the earth.
- **Mulch** - Material that consists of broken down bark, leaves, and compost, to put over the soil to enrich it. This often looks like dirt.
- **Cover crop** - These are different from the crops you will harvest because cover crops are planted with the purpose of covering the soil to protect it and enrich it.
- **Deadheading** - The process of removing dead flower heads from the stems.
- **Pinching** - A technique that is used to create more stems by pinching the main stem with your fingers. This causes pruning and encourages more branching.
- **Direct sow** - Is just another way to say the term direct seeding. It means to plant seeds directly

into the soil rather than start with a plant or start inside with the seeds.

- **Full sun** - With full sun a plant will need at least six hours of direct sunlight a day to grow and bloom.
- **Partial sun** - Can also be referred to as partial shade. It means that a plant will need three to six hours of direct sun per day.
- **Germination** - This is when the seed starts to grow into a seedling. This occurs right after dormancy and is the beginning of the process.
- **Hardening off** - The process of allowing a plant to transition from a protected greenhouse environment to the outdoors where sun, wind, and other harsher elements will be exposed.
- **Native** - These plants are the natural landscape of the area that has developed over hundreds of years due to the soil and climate of the area.
- **Pollination** - This is the transfer of pollen to the flower as a way of fertilizing the plant.
- **Self-sow** - Plants that drop seeds and replant themselves are called self-sowing plants. They essentially start the gardening process on their own.
- **Thinning** - The process of cutting/snipping back seedlings that have more than one or two sets of true leaves.

- **Transplanting** - This is when you move a plant to the correct space in a garden or you put a new already bought plant in the garden.

## THE SECRET IS IN THE SOIL

The cliche quote about having a solid foundation being the key to a good home, a successful marriage, and so on, can also apply to your garden. Growing vegetables requires nutritious and healthy soil that they can thrive in with the correct PH levels, moisture, and natural ingredients.

A common mistake (one that everyone makes in the beginning) is to try and plant and sow in soil that just isn't ready. We skip right to the vegetables and forget to make a good home for them first. That's why understanding what type of soil you are working with and how to get it ready is key. Let's take a look at the different situations you may be dealing with.

### Find Out Your Soil Type

Understanding Point A is going to help you get to Point B. Your Point A is the soil type you are working with and Point B is the soil type you need. We can categorize six different types of soil that are common to cross paths with.

Here they are:

1. **Silty Soil** - This can also be commonly referred to as Silt. Silty soil is often described as light and retains moisture particularly well. Because it also drains well it can be very slippery when wet and wash away. It's not grainy due to its fine particle makeup and will not retain its shape for a long period of time if you roll it into a ball.

2. **Sandy Soil** - This soil is free draining and can dry out very quickly when the weather gets warm. When it rains, it also leaks out its nutrients letting them wash away. It's gritty so when it is wet it can roll into a ball well. But when it dries out it crumbles easily. In order to be suitable for plants, it needs a lot of additional organic matter.

3. **Peaty Soil** - Peaty Soil is one of the more acidic soils and contains a lot of organic matter. The downside to this type of soil is that it is relatively low in nutrients and can become waterlogged easily. It's not common to find this soil in gardens but certain flowers like Azalea love it. It's a dark and spongy type of soil that you can ball up.

4. **Loamy Soil** - If you are looking for a perfect soil type to work with this is it. It's not free-draining and also doesn't get waterlogged. It warms quickly in the spring while also providing your vegetables with a lot of nutrients. The reason it is so perfect is that it is a mixture of clay, silt, and sand soils and has different-sized particles. It does roll into a ball easily but doesn't keep its shape as well as some of the others.

5. **Clay Soil** - Clay has the same properties as molding clay. It can become super dry and hard after warming up slowly and then cracks. It does not drain well and is incredibly hard to work with and dig up. While not ideal for gardening, it does have a lot of nutrients and can retain its shape when rolled up in a ball well.

6. **Chalky Soil** - This type of soil usually lies over chalk or limestone bedrock resulting in very gritty soil. It is alkaline soil that is also free-draining and has a lot of bigger stones and particles. While it is nutrient-rich it also leaches out its most helpful nutrients such as manganese and iron when wet. Adding a good amount of fertilizer can sometimes be the solution here.

*How to Test Your PH Levels*

As a gardener, it is incredibly important to know what kind of PH levels you are working with when it comes to your soil. Anything that is too acidic or not acidic enough can result in frustration and a garden that lacks vegetable growth. It's also important to know which vegetables have specific PH levels that they thrive in.

The scale ranges from zero to fourteen, with zero being extremely acidic and fourteen being extremely alkaline. Typically, most soils in the U.S. will fall somewhere between 6.0-7.0 PH levels. You can test the level with a pre-bought PH Level Testing Kit or use a homemade kit.

The pre-bought kits are self-explanatory, with testing strips and easy-to-follow directions right on the package. But if you know the vinegar and baking soda trick, there is no need to spend extra money.

**DIY With Baking Soda and Vinegar**

 You can also save the video instructions to refer back to later.

**Total Time:**

15 Minutes

**Ingredient List:**

- Two small plastic containers
- Trowel (small shovel)
- White vinegar
- Baking soda

**Directions:**

1. The first step is getting a sample batch of soil and putting it in the container. You will want to take soil from a few different areas in the garden or space you plan on planting. This is because one area could have higher levels of acid than others and blending different areas can help you get a better overall picture.
2. Now, you will first test for alkalinity. You will need to add ½ cup of water to the soil and container and mix it around. Next, you will add a ½ cup of vinegar to the container. Pay close attention and look to see if there is a fizzing or bubbling film after adding the vinegar. If yes, then you have alkaline soil. The more bubbling film the more alkalinity it has.

3. Next, you will test for acidity. Use a new soil batch, repeating the first step and putting it into a container. First, add a ½ cup of water to the soil and mix. Now you will add a ½ cup of baking soda to the container. If you get a bubbling film or fizzling soil then it is acidic. Again the more reaction you get the more acidic it is.

4. When you have PH levels that are too acidic or alkaline, then you will need to amend the soil to bring it back to a PH level that works for the plants. Normally, plants thrive in a slightly acidic setting. There are different things you can mix into the soil to bring the PH level up or down.

   a) To raise the acid levels, you can incorporate pine needles into the soil. You can also pour coffee grounds into the soil to raise the levels quickly and easily.
   b) To raise the alkalinity you can mix in wood ashes or agricultural lime.

By following these steps you can successfully prepare and understand the soil type you are working with and how to make it suitable for your garden.

*Alternate Tips for Amending Your Soil*

Coffee grounds and pine needles are great for amending your soil but most don't realize it is not a one-time job. You will want to constantly amend your soil over time to keep it fresh. The best way to do this is to use organic matter. The best organic matter is compost.

Since water is alkaline you can combat this by watering plants with compost tea. This doesn't necessarily mean dumping a teapot on your plants. Try out this trick.

Sit a five-gallon bucket of water out in the sun for twenty-four hours. This will get rid of access to chlorine. Next, you can dump five to ten cups of compost tea into the mix. Let it sit for forty-eight hours and stir periodically. Strain the compost and place the liquid into a watering can to water your plants!

## PATIENCE IS VIRTUE

After reading this first chapter, you are probably feeling mixed emotions. It may feel like it is a lot to take in at first or it may feel very exciting to have the knowledge to finally start out on the right foot. Maybe both! That's OK because this chapter should be used as your reference guide that you can come back to over and over again. Mastering the basics takes time and normally we need to have a few uh-ohs before we can really feel comfortable with what we are doing.

The most important thing is to really understand the foundation of soil. It plays a role in how successful the final product turns out every single time. Knowing what type of soil we have and deciphering the PH levels is key. Luckily, this is not a difficult process to go through. Then we can finally move on to amending our soil and thinking about the types of plants we want to have.

Let's continue this journey with the idea in mind that gardening requires a lot of patience. The better we understand that the more enjoyable the process will be. Let's get gardening!

# 2

# THE ESSENTIALS OF COMPOST

We've talked a little bit now about soil types and why it's so important to have great soil before starting to plant your vegetables. But there is another common mistake that many of us make along the way. It's been ingrained in us through great marketing that there are a number of fertilizers and magic products that can make your veggies big, beautiful, and tasty. While that may be true for some, I am a firm believer that you don't need to feed your plants for them to get the nutrients they need. Starting from the ground up, you can take care of your soil with compost making it nutrient-dense. From there the soil will give those nutrients to your plants in a natural and healthy way.

Now, I am not saying that the soil does the gardening for you. I am just saying sometimes the best things in life are free and purchasing the right fertilizer may not be the best solution for your plants. That's why in this chapter, we need to learn the essentials of compost and what makes it such a great option for your plants but also a financially beneficial and environmentally friendly choice.

## WHY EVERYONE SHOULD BE COMPOSTING

A part of me thinks that if you are into gardening, you have a connection with this earth. For some, it may be more potent than others. Regardless, knowing that composting has a super beneficial impact on our world and environment is reason alone to do it! Interestingly, food and yard waste comprise 30 percent of the total household waste. Bringing this kind of a waste to a landfill doesn't decompose properly because it doesn't have the necessary elements to do so. Worse is how it decays and adds to the existing greenhouse gas.

While this is not a book on global warming, it makes sense that we should use this 30 percent of compost and put it to a cause that actually needs it! When we use this for our gardens, plants are actually getting what they need from a natural source rather than man-made fertilizers.

Here are a few easy-to-understand benefits of composting.

- Your plants and vegetables are going to be much happier with organic nutrients.
- Composting suppresses pests and diseases that could otherwise kill your crop.
- Eliminates the need for chemical fertilizers that can be dangerous to children and pets.
- It helps leave a lighter carbon footprint

## WHAT MATERIALS CAN WE COMPOST?

We must understand what we can and can't compost because some materials do not disintegrate naturally and will ruin your soil. If you start to work with compost and find yourself making a few errors along the way, it's OK. I'll start by telling you about my own garden flop before moving on to let you experience yours. When you read things online and think, "Well, a milk mask is good for your skin," you believe suddenly milk must be suitable for everything. I started throwing dairy into my compost because before learning the details, I just figured all food breaks down, so it shall go into my compost.

Before I knew it, I had all the dairy products in the world thrown into my compost and altering my garden.

It smelled gross, but I thought, what compost would smell good? It was surprising to find a lot of creepy crawlers eating the vegetables that I was planning to eat myself! They got there first. Only later did I realize that dairy is a big no-no for composting for this exact reason.

Let's start with what we can compost because that list is easy to identify.

### The Nitrogen Carbon Combo

The secret formula that we can come back to over and over again is greens, browns, and water. But it's not as simple as just throwing that all together. The first step in thinking about what we can compost is somewhat understanding what type of compost mechanism we have. Some systems will work better than others. Having said that, the focus needs to be on having the right balance of nitrogen-based products and carbon-based products.

**Rule To Remember:** Compost should have a lot more carbon than nitrogen. Because the browns usually have less nitrogen than greens you can work with ⅔ brown materials to ⅓ green.

Some people say you want a healthy mix of greens and browns. It's easy to get confused because it contradicts the former general rule. The reason being is that we can get very technical with some types of greens and browns that will give off more carbon or nitrogen than we want. So, let's talk about the nitty-gritty.

## Too Much Carbon

It's important to know what too much carbon looks like because you want to be able to fix your mistakes the next time you compost. When you have too much carbon, it may just take longer to compose. In general, most people will tell you when in doubt, put more carbon in.

## Too Much Nitrogen

The same cannot be said for having too much nitrogen. Too much nitrogen can definitely ruin your compost. It becomes too dense and oftentimes will give a very unpleasant odor. It becomes a fire risk because technically speaking it can combust.

## Browns And Carbon

- Wood Chips
- Wood Ash
- Shrub Prunings
- Sawdust Pellets
- Pine Needles
- Dead leaves

- Coffee Grounds
- Dryer Lint (technically not brown)
- Cardboard

**Greens and Nitrogen**

- Flower Cuttings
- Green Leaves
- Lawn and Garden Weeds
- Seaweed or Kelp

Keep in mind that other household items like newspapers, table scraps, and some foods are also great resources to add to your compost pile. These are just some common examples you can find around the house.

## WHAT CAN'T BE COMPOSTED

So, now we have a general idea of what can be composted, but it's still important to understand what can't be composted. Or else you may end up with a dairy disaster, as I did! Here is some food for thought:

1. Stay away from things that attract bugs. This includes meat and fish as well as poultry. Even bones with leftover scents can be problematic

and ruin your compost, thanks to unwanted visitors.

2. Diseased plants can end up spreading to the rest of your compost and altering the level of nitrogen and carbon. It can also ruin your existing plants if you try to take this compost and put it back in your garden.

3. You may see something like chicken manure on some lists. But truth be told, you should stay away from animal manure if you plan to use this compost for soil that works with food.

4. Another thing that can commonly attract pests is fruit peels. Because of the sweetness, anything like a banana peel, orange, peel, etc may not be a great idea. Same for an apple core or anything similar.

5. Black walnut leaves can't be composted. These contain toxic chemicals that can ruin your garden. The same can be said for coal or charcoal ash, as they also contain harmful properties.

Again consider these to be some of the general rules, and if you ever doubt whether an item can or can't be composted, a quick Google search can solve the issue in a matter of seconds.

## HOW TO START COMPOSTING AT HOME TODAY!

A consistent theme we will see throughout this book is that you don't need to be an expert at anything to get started. The same things can definitely be said when it comes to starting your compost. There are many different ways to start composting, but some are more complicated such as a three-box system. For now, I want to share some of the more suitable options for beginners so we can set ourselves up for success.

### *The Container Method*

There are two options when it comes to using a container. First, we can explain all the steps with the container that contains holes. Then we can follow the same protocols with a container that has its base cut out from underneath.

### **What You Need**

- A 50L plastic trash container
- Compost materials
- A grassy and shady area

## Step-By-Step Instructions

1. Take your trash bin and punch holes all around it while separating them about three inches apart. There should be holes around the base of the trash bin as well as vertically up and down the sides. This is to allow for proper drainage and aeration. The size is also important because you want to be able to fit a good chunk of compostable materials in there.

2. The first batch of materials that should go into your compost bin is twigs and straw. Order matters here as these two materials closest to the bottom of the barrel will help aerate it and keep the drainage system working as needed. You can pile this up a few inches high in the barrel.

3. Here is where we consider the perfect combination of carbon and nitrogen as well as enough air and water. Incorporate your combination of greens and browns with the carbon rule in mind. For any materials that are larger or tough to break down, you will want to help the process move faster by breaking it down as small as possible first.

4. Whenever you decide to add new materials to the compost (you most likely will weekly), it's

important to bury these items right underneath the top layer. This helps them decompose faster. You also want to spend time mixing all the materials once a week to ensure they are getting good access to air. If your compost starts to look dry, you can go ahead and add water.

5. After a few months, you will notice that your compost is ready! It turns a very dark brown and begins to look like it blends right in with the earth. There is probably a little bit of an odor to it and will be warm to touch. This is normal because there are microbes living inside of it.

This is the easiest way to start your compost. But you can also go right ahead and cut the entire bottom of the barrel out. This helps the compost come into contact with the earth directly. There is a lot of benefit to this and is a good alternative if you don't want to cut a lot of holes out.

### Getting Started Today

As you can see, composting really is like throwing the kitchen sink at the earth. While it may have sounded complicated at first, it is a really easy process to get started that doesn't take a whole lot of effort. Having said that, not everyone has the patience to wait six to nine months. If you are one of those people and your soil really looks like it could use some help, there is organic compost for sale.

It is rewarding to have control over your own compost. The environmental benefits are great and your garden will be thankful, too. Being free of any harmful fertilizers to help the soil will not only help your vegetables but also prevent yourself from interacting with chemicals as well. Just remember that while the process is exciting not everything is meant to be composted.

It's easy to justify that just because twigs and other food groups are compostable that similar items can go in as well. But as we learned from our list of do not's there are actually quite a few items that shouldn't go in your barrel. The last thing we need is chemicals going back into our garden or attracting all sorts of pests and bugs! With this chapter as a nice and easy reference guide, you can start getting your compost going today!

# 3

# YOUR GARDEN DESIGN: FROM GROW BAGS TO RAISED BEDS

Now we are getting closer to the actual planting of our vegetables. But it takes some time to think about where the best places in our yard will be for our garden. We have a lot of different considerations, such as the sun, and hardiness zones, among other factors. All these factors put together to create an environment that will allow your vegetable garden to succeed the best.

We also have to take into consideration the many different ways to design your garden in terms of using grow bags, raised beds, or any of the other methods that are easy for beginners to pick up and learn. For me, I have moved my garden around a few times because I couldn't quite figure out the tricks and didn't have any valuable tips beforehand. Moving a garden is not easy because you must prepare all the soil again, so take my mistakes and learn from them.

Let's start with how we can map out a garden design for success!

## SUN GAZING

My first error was underestimating just how much sun my vegetables and garden needed. Many different kinds of vegetables are going to call for different sun recipes, as I like to call them. But the technical terms are full sun and partial sun. In order to understand what parts of your yard area get sun and light, you will need to pay close attention to where the sun hits and how much sun and shade there is in different areas throughout the day. You can do this by cutting your yard into different sections.

You will also want to pay attention to how the sun changes during the seasons if you plan on growing for spring, summer, and fall. Ultimately, mark the area's full sun and partial sun on a piece of paper.

## HOW IMPORTANT ARE U.S. HARDINESS ZONES

If you are an avid plant shopper like I am, then you will have likely come across the terminology U.S. hardiness zone. If not, now is a great chance to fully understand it because it has a decent impact on how our gardens turn out. The United States Department of Agriculture uses historical data of weather temperatures to divide our country into twelve different zones that are referenced by number and letter. The scale has a range from one (being the coldest) to thirteen (being the warmest). Then either the letter A or B is tagged onto the number to further divide the groups, with A being the coldest and B being the warmest.

But why do we need to know this?

As gardeners, we can look up our own hardiness zones to understand what types of vegetables and plants are going to do the best in our climates. Some vegetables are considered warm-weather vegetables, just as others are considered cool-tolerant veggies. All we have to do is understand what our zone is, and then we can see just how easy or difficult it is to plant certain vegetables.

## All Fifty States

To make things just a little easier, here are the hardiness zones for everywhere in the United States. You will see that states have multiple zones because, of course, they have a range of different weather conditions. Some states, like Texas and California, need to be divided up because of their size.

- Alabama - 7a through 9a
- Alaska - 1a through 8b
- Arizona - 4b through 10b
- Arkansas - 6b through 8a
- California North - 5a through 10b
- California South - 5a through 11a
- Colorado - 7a through 8a
- Connecticut - 5b through 7a
- Delaware - 7a and 7b
- District of Columbia - 5b through 8a
- Florida - 8a through 11a
- Georgia - 6a through 9a
- Hawaii - 9a though 13a
- Idaho - 3b through 7b
- Illinois - 5a through 7a
- Indiana - 5b through 6b
- Iowa - 4b through 6a
- Kansas - 3b through 7a

- Kentucky - 6a through 7a
- Louisiana - 8a through 10a
- Maine - 3b through 6a
- Maryland - 5b through 8a
- Massachusetts - 5a through 7b
- Michigan - 4a through 6b
- Minnesota - 3a through 5a
- Mississippi - 7b through 9a
- Missouri - 5b through 7b
- Montana - 3a through 6a
- Nebraska - 4a through 5b
- Nevada - 4a through 10a
- New Hampshire - 3b through 6a
- New Jersey - 6a through 7b
- New Mexico - 4b through 9a
- New York - 3b through 7b
- North Carolina - 5b through 8b
- North Dakota - 3a through 4b
- Ohio - 5b through 6b
- Oklahoma - 6a through 8a
- Oregon - 4b through 9b
- Pennsylvania - 5a through 7b
- Rhode Island - 5b through 7a
- South Carolina - 7a through 9a
- South Dakota - 3b through 5b
- Tennessee - 5b through 8a
- Texas East - 7b through 10a

- Texas West - 6b through 9a
- Utah - 4a through 9a
- Vermont - 3b through 5b
- Virginia - 5a through 8a
- Washington - 4a through 9a
- West Virginia - 5a through 7a
- Wisconsin - 3b through 5b
- Wyoming - 3a through 6a

 But it's not enough to just know the range you are in. That's why using the official USDA website to check your specific hardiness zone is crucial. You can go to the website by scanning the code below.

***Other Considerations***

The USDA map to tell you your local area's hardiness is a really great tool for beginners who need to familiarize themselves with gardening and different plants and vegetables. Having said that, there are quite a few different considerations that the USDA Hardiness score does not account for.

Wind, humidity, and snow are just a few things that can dramatically change the temperature and condition in which the plant thrives. Because the temperature is also an average, there is no consideration for exposure to cold temperatures. The day may warm up quickly, but being exposed to cold for too long of a time can kill the plants. The best way to see how you can confirm how well your vegetable or plants will do is to do some local research. Likely, you have friends or neighbors nearby that have experimented.

## VEGETABLE GARDEN DESIGN IDEAS

Regardless of where you live and the temperatures or climates you have to deal with, there are many different options for growing your vegetables. Different design ideas work for different reasons, which is why we can have a brief overview of the more common approaches to gardening. Sometimes, combining a few different designs makes the best garden and the process a little more fun.

*Raised Beds*

We spent some time discussing how to prepare your soil for planting. Now lets understand not all planting has to be dug right into the ground. Raised beds are structures that provide a framework or enclosure, usually six to eight inches high so you can garden above the ground. They can be aesthetically pleasing while also serving the purpose of providing a potentially longer growing season. They warm up quickly and provide great draining systems.

**When to Use:**

The best situation to use raised beds is when you have marshy yards or areas that are prone to a lot of flooding. This can drown your vegetables, because they offer a great drainage system, this protects them. They also are convenient because you won't have as many weeds or crabgrass growing out of them. This is easier maintenance.

### *Hanging Planters*

Typically speaking, hanging planters or baskets are meant for design purposes. They are suspended planters that usually hold flowers and add some greenery to the space. However, having said that, some creative individuals have used them before for herbs or other vegetable garden needs.

**When to Use:**

Hanging planters are great for indoor gardening. Of course, we still need to take a look at how much light and sun the plants get, but it's an alternative for those who don't have any outdoor space. But they can be used outdoors as well and are perfect for apartments with decks or balconies.

### Containers For Tight Squeezes

Not everyone has a lot of garden space, so using containers can actually be a great idea. There are a lot of different shapes and sizes, but you may see them offer just a little pot space for each separate plant or vegetable. Again, these are best for smaller plants.

**When to Use:**

Containers, as mentioned, are also great for tight spaces and provide some of the same benefits as hanging planters. This is also one of the easiest ways to work with soil and control any sort of pest problem that may occur with in-ground gardening.

## *Grow Bags*

Grow bags are larger bags that allow us to plant small to medium vegetables and flowers. You will find a lot of them to be made out of plastic, but some are offered in breathable plastic. They are great for plants that don't have deep roots and offer a solution for those who can't have an in-ground garden.

**When to Use:**

Grow bags are easy to use and a very convenient option even if you do have a lot of space. They also attract pollinators which brings a whole new layer of convenience to your gardening. The roots also behave differently compared to plastic container gardening. Many have found that grow bags are a more natural solution for plants to evolve.

### Greenhouses

Greenhouses are an excellent option for those with a lot of space and some money to build one. They allow for year-round gardening and the ability to control a lot of factors. However, mini-greenhouses are also becoming popular for those who don't have as much space. Typically they are no more than ten square feet and can even be man-made.

**When to Use:**

Greenhouses, as mentioned, are for those who may have a little more space, time, and money. But, ultimately, they are great for those who really want to commit to gardening long-term because it allows for you to do it much more frequently.

## MAPPING YOUR GARDEN OUT

Imagine walking out your back door and looking over your beautiful backyard. There is so much space to choose from, we don't even know where to start. Start by zoning your backyard, as mentioned, with partial and full sun areas. We also are going to use the method that starts us at our backdoor and moves us farther away. This means considering vegetables that are going to need daily care and attention. They will go closest to our back door because they will likely need daily watering. Then the vegetables that are less "needy" can be farther away.

In the next chapters, we can take a closer look at what vegetables will need more attention and how you should care for different groups. While we do this, we should always keep in mind that there is no perfect solution to a garden design. It's always a great idea to be thoughtful with our process but we will encounter potential issues with every situation. In addition, our gardens have their own microclimates, which means they are not one-size-fits-all.

Whether you have an interest in using grow bags or hanging planters, there are many different situations to fill different needs. Sometimes, a garden can use a combination to be most creative with your space. But ultimately, a greenhouse or even a mini greenhouse will always offer you the most flexibility year-round because of the layer of protection it provides from the elements.

Now that we have an idea of what we need to start a vegetable garden and how we can prepare a proper home for our veggies, it's finally time to start learning how to plant specific vegetable families.

# 4

# THE BRASSICAS FAMILY

To some this vegetable family is known officially as the Brassicas family. However, when I started playing around with these vegetables they were simply the Mustard family. Officially, the name is Brassica

Oleracea and can be classified as cruciferous vegetables. If you are thinking what I am thinking then you may be wondering why all the names and do they matter? Yes! It's actually good to get acquainted with the different names because this is one of the most popular vegetable families and is referenced differently all the time. Throwing just one more at you, it's also called the Cabbage family!

In this chapter, we can talk about why this vegetable family is a must for your garden. The health benefits just blew me away and it truly is one of the most popular vegetable families grown all over the world. Can you guess what some of these veggies are? Now if you love sushi you'll be excited to know that Wasabi is a part of this gang. But for those who don't love spicy, don't worry. Fan favorites like brussel sprouts and broccoli also stand strong in this group.

Since I love a good turnip let's turn it up and get talking about the benefits. Ok, no more corn-y vegetable jokes, I promise!

## WHAT IS THE BRASSICAS FAMILY?

The Brassicas family has quite literally hundreds of subspecies making it a very large family. We see some of the most common vegetables in this group such as cabbage, broccoli, collard greens, and so much more. Some of the reasons it's such a popular bunch is because it's relatively easy to harvest and they have some of the most nutritious values out of all our vegetable friends.

So it may be a little more obvious why the family is often referred to as the Cabbage family but where does the Mustard family come from? Well, the mustard seeds that come from these plants can be crushed and then mixed together with vinegar, water, or other liquids and create mustard. After planting some tomatoes, you'll have nearly all the ingredients and condiments for a perfect summer cheeseburger. But that's just one of many benefits.

### Taking Advantage of the Many Benefits

It's worth taking a look at some of the benefits that come from the Cabbage family because, ultimately, growing veggies is a lot of dedicated time and hard work. Understanding what you get out of it just makes it that much more pleasurable.

### Rich in Vitamin C and E

Brassica vegetables are incredibly high in vitamins and minerals. The first two vitamins that come to mind are Vitamin C and Vitamin E. This contributes to low blood pressure. Vitamin E contributes to positive brain function and lowers your risk of Alzheimer's. They also have a pretty significant range of calcium resulting in strong bones. Potassium is another mineral that is fairly evident, playing a role in having a great metabolism.

## Plenty of Carotenoids

These plentiful antioxidants get converted into Vitamin A by our bodies. Which helps us have healthy eyes and healthy skin. Antioxidants also have a great impact on our immune system. When it comes to vegetables and carotenoids, we see high levels in broccoli. We also see this in kale, but if you eat two cups raw, then you actually have more than the daily recommended intake of Vitamin A by the FDA.

## Bring on Some Folate

Folate is also considered to be Vitamin B9 and helps with the growth of red and white blood cells. This contributes to healthy cell function and can be positive for pregnant women. In addition, it helps lower the risk of birth defects, so this is a natural way to increase your intake.

## Fiber

Fiber can be difficult to get without eating carbs. However, these are healthy carbs and a great source of fiber. Fiber can help you curb cravings with fewer calories in this instance. It also improves your gut health.

## TOP TEN BRASSICA VEGETABLES TO GROW

With all these benefits listed, it's not hard to imagine you are ready to start growing and planting this vegetable family. But even though they are from the same family, they have different requirements. So let's break down each of these top ten brassica vegetables so we can set ourselves up for success and a healthy harvest.

### *Turnips*

If you love a good soup or stew, turnips are the perfect solution. These root vegetables are fall-planted annuals providing harvest in the fall and winter. They are hardy vegetables that should be sown directly into the soil.

But because they are an annual, you will need to replant them every year. Technically speaking, you can plant them in spring, but they should never be planted in the summer. Staggering your planting every ten days will provide a continual harvest

**How to Plant:**

1. Five weeks before the last frost date is when you need to start planting them for springtime. For fall, five weeks before the first frost date is when to sow.
2. They can withstand the cold weather. If you are looking to use the whole turnip, plant in a full sun area to get six to eight hours a day. If you want just the leaves, partial sun will work.
3. Plant your seedlings about a ½ each deep with one inch apart in a row. The rows should be placed one foot from each other, giving space for the roots to grow—cover seedlings with soil.
4. Once you see your seedlings, thin your soil to every four inches. Here is when you also need to check to see how the soil moisture is as a dry root will result in a dried-out turnip.

### Radishes

Radishes are very similar to turnips in the sense that they are hardy root veggies. These vegetables are great because they have multiple harvest times and can be ready as quickly as three weeks.

They are also annuals, so you'll need to stagger plant seeds just like the turnips. You can plant in both the fall and spring but never sow in warmer temperatures (70 Fahrenheit and up) just like turnips. However, they do need six hours of full sun every day and should be watered frequently without becoming waterlogged.

*Tip: Place radishes near your turnips as they are a great pest deter, and turnips happen to attract pests!*

**How to Plant:**

1. Spring plantings should be four to six weeks before the last spring frost, and for fall, sow seeds four to six weeks before the first fall frost.
2. Add your organic compost to the ground and sow seeds at ½ inch deep while pushing a light layer of soil over them. Seeds should be sown one inch apart with your rows one foot apart making it the exact same as turnips.
3. While providing water to your seedlings, keep an eye out for when they get to be about two inches tall or one week old. This is when you need to thin them. Thin your radishes to three inches apart, so they don't crowd each other.
4. Save your snippings as these greens are edible and can easily be tossed as a garnish or on a

salad. It's also important to weed along with thinning so they don't get overcrowded.

5. When harvesting approaches, there are two things to keep in mind: Check the seed packet because different radishes have different timing. Also, don't leave them in the ground too long past maturity! You can take it out of the ground when the top part is poking through the soil.

## Kale

Kale is one of the most popular vegetables used in salads and a number of dishes all over the world now. Kale is a little different, being that it's really neither an annual or perennial. It can be best classified as a biennial but grown as an annual or perennial. Woah. Let's talk about this. Kale thrones in a nitrogen setting and will really love organic compost. Luckily, it can be sown in both the fall and spring.

**How to Plant:**

1. Kale should be sown directly five weeks before the last expected spring frost or until six weeks before the first frost for the fall. While you will get plentiful crops, many agree fall is better than spring for flavor.

2. Baby kale will require these spacing dimensions: Sow one inch apart in trenches spaced four inches apart. Kale for cooking will follow these spacing dimensions: Sow twelve inches apart for smaller varieties and eighteen inches apart for larger ones.

3. All seeds will be sown 1/4 to ½ inches deep where it can get a full five hours of direct sun each day.

### Cabbage

Since cabbage is a cool-weather crop, it is best to plant this one in the spring so you can have it for summer! You aren't just limited to that harvesting season, though. You can also harvest late summer to take advantage of fall and winter recipes. Cabbages are annual and will need six hours of full sun per day. Interestingly enough, we can start this growing process indoors!

**How to Plant:**

1. Start your seed indoors between four and six weeks before the first spring frost. This is because cabbage has a long growing season and will not need to be sowed until the soil is worked in the spring.

2. Sow the seeds ½ inch deep with 1-inch spacing apart from each other. When thinning starts, you will want to thin them to 18 inches to 24 inches apart.

3. When the soil softens enough to work with, ensure you use a rich organic compost with a lot of nitrogen to nourish the cabbage outside properly. Cabbage works best in a soil pH between 6.5 to 6.8 with the exception of 7.0 if there is a disease problem.

4. When the cabbage shows four to five true leaves or becomes around four to five weeks old, you can transplant them outdoors with 18 to 24 inches in space. The rows should also have 24 to 36 inches in between to not crowd them.

5. Once they have found their space, you will want to bury the stem one to two inches deep. The two top sets of leaves will be poking out.

6. Water your cabbages 1 to 1 ½ inches evenly every week—1 inch results in 16 gallons for perspective.

Cabbage has a big range when it comes to harvesting. They can be ready 80 to 180 days after seeding. When the head is firm, and the base is 4 to 10 inches in size, you can cut and harvest them.

### Mustard Greens

Mustard greens give a little kick of flavor to every meal. They are annual and need new seeds down each year. Expect them to need six to eight hours of full sun each day and follow a similar path as the others! This means planting in early spring or late summer.

**How to Plant:**

1. Sow your seeds directly into the soil just ¼ inch deep and one inch apart. Lightly cover soil over. They will only take a few days to germinate.
2. Water the mustard greens two inches weekly and evenly to keep the soil well hydrated. It would be best if you also continued to keep weeds out, so they don't coed the greens during the growing process.
3. Mustard greens grow quickly and can be harvested as baby mustard greens just twenty to thirty days later. For mature mustard greens, you are looking at forty days.
4. Snip off the outermost leaves to harvest and also to keep the soil's growing point intact. When you do this, you can count on multiple harvests!

## *Cauliflower*

Cauliflower crust pizza is so much more satisfying when it comes from your own garden. This annual presents slightly more of a challenge than its friends. Plan on planting these guys a week or two before the last frost in spring or in late summer for a fall harvest. Count on also giving it six hours of fun sun each day!

**How to Plant:**

1. Use a nice moist, rich in nitrogen, organic matter for planting cauliflower with a pH level between 6.0 and 7.0 for best results. Cauliflower is a bit needier to ensure you take care of your soil. It should be consistent at eight to ten inches in depth.

2. You can start seedlings indoors for six weeks and transplant or sow directly into the soil just after the last frost date. For this purpose, we will start from the seedlings in the ground.

3. Seedlings should be transplanted with space 18 inches apart and rows spaced 40 inches apart. Make sure to give the seedlings water immediately if transplanted. They also will need one inch of water weekly.

*Broccoli*

Broccoli is actually a biennial crop but confuses people when it acts as an annual because of its short season. Staying consistent with your family members, you need six hours of full sun each day. In addition, your soil needs to be nitrogen-rich and aim for a pH scale from 6.0 to 7.0.

**How to Plant:**

1. Besides having the pH levels right you also need an area with great drainage. If this means using raised beds, definitely consider it.
2. Compost matter needs to integrate into the soil roughly one week before you plan on transplanting or sowing the seeds.
3. Sow your seeds 1/2 inch deep with three inches of space in between. If you are transplanting seedlings, give more space such as 12 inches. The row should have 3 feet in between.
4. Water 1 ½ inches weekly to keep the mulch and soil moist. The water needs to be around the base and not the head to prevent rot from being soggy.
5. Expect not to harvest your broccoli before eighty days. Sometimes it even takes 100 days. When you do go to harvest, the flowers should

be just ready to bloom. In this case, you can cut at a diagonal with a sharp knife. You want to try to include about six inches.

## Brussel Sprouts

Brussel sprouts are a personal favorite, and you have to admit they've become very trendy. They are also biennials even if grown as annuals. They are best sown in the fall, but you can harvest for the summer if you want to start in early spring. Expect for them to need six hours of full sun. They have a harvesting range from eighty to thirty days.

### How to Plant:

1. Sow your seeds about 3 to 4 inches apart unless you work with seedlings. Seedlings need to be planted 18-24 inches apart.
2. From the moment you plant, the soil should also be moist, which means watering frequently. It should never be soggy.
3. Brussels germinate easily and are relatively easy to care for. Once they have two sets of leaves, this is the time to start thinning them 1-2 foot spacing.
4. They are typically ready to harvest when they are one to two inches in diameter. You want to

start from the bottom of the plant and work your way to the top. You also can snip off the leaves that develop around the sprouts.

## Watercress

Surprisingly, watercress is a part of this family. This is a perennial plant and is one of the easiest ones to grow! Watercress does best when it has four hours of full sun and then shade for the rest of the day.

### How to Plant:

1. Consider sowing the seed three weeks before the last frost-free date, about ¼ inch deep, just under the surface of the soil.
2. This is an aquatic plant so watering two to three inches so the soil is submerged and kept wet is the idea.
3. Since it can take just three weeks to harvest, cut the stems at about four inches with clean tools.

## Bok Choy

Bok Choy may be last on our list but it is not the least. It has some of the best nutritional benefits. This biennial plant can be grown in spring, late summer, or fall even though it's a cool-tolerant vegetable. It actually does great in three to five hours of partial shade.

**How to Plant:**

1. Make sure that your nutrient-rich soil is able to drain well. This is not like watercress and you want to make sure you don't drown the plant.
2. You want to plant your seed two inches apart from each other and there is no need to cover the seeds with a lot of soil. A little will do. You also want to make sure your rows are 10 inches apart.
3. Eventually, you will thin them to eight inches apart. When the bok choy starts to reach 12 inches to 18 inches, this is an indicator that it's ready to harvest. This is about forty-five days after sowing.
4. To harvest, slice the plant about 1 inch from the ground.

A GREAT PLACE TO START

We start with this family because gardening follows the same process as picking up any other hobby. You don't want to challenge yourself with the most difficult things to grow. It's better to start with the basics and then work with relatively easy vegetables with lower maintenance. They are all cool-tolerant vegetables that grow relatively fast. Having said that, I have had my fair share of trial and error even with these vegetables.

Whether they bolt because of warm weather or pests have decided to harvest them first, there are always mistakes to be made. That's why really paying close attention to your soil and sun can make a huge difference in your gardening success!

# Please Leave a Review!

Dear Valued Readers,
We hope you have enjoyed and benefited from the content we bring to you. As authors, we pour our hearts and souls into creating engaging and thought-provoking pieces that resonate with you. Today, we would like to kindly ask for a moment of your time to consider leaving a review about our work. Your reviews hold immense significance for us as authors. They provide valuable insight into what aspects of our writing resonate with you and what areas we can improve upon. Therefore, by leaving a review, you contribute to our growth and success. We sincerely appreciate your support and the time you invest in sharing your thoughts. Thank you for your time.
Warmest regards,
Noor Fatima

# 5

# THE LEAFY GREENS

L eafy greens happen to be a personal favorite because I love salads. We have already come into play with some salad greens but many of these leafy greens fall under different families. The two other vegetable families that we can take a look at are the Amaranthaceae and Asteraceae. Yes, it took me a long time to learn how to pronounce that, too. Why can't they make these names easier?

Leafy greens are rich in benefits especially when it comes to Vitamin A and Vitamin K. Always remember the more colorful or bold our greens look the better they are for you. Let's not forget about Vitamin C, the fiber, and Vitamin B. There is just so much to love about these guys and even if you don't love them, you'll be thankful to have them around.

### WHAT IS CLASSED AS A LEAFY GREEN?

The first step is really to understand what a leafy green is. You may take some common guesses in spinach, kale, and lettuce. While those are all right, the leafy greens family (Aster) has 20,000 different species. Here we can talk about eleven of our favorites. But it's important to understand that leafy greens aren't just vegetables. Oddly enough, lettuce is related to dandelion, ragweed, and a number of flowers. Something most have in common is the leaves they have hanging off their stems. They come in all shapes, sizes, and colors from fuchsia to dark green, so leafy greens don't always necessarily mean just green.

*The Aster Family Benefits*

As we know, this is one of the largest plant families all over the world. While they also have a great deal of Vitamin C, Vitamin B is prevalent as well. There is also a good amount of niacin and thiamin. This improves brain function and helps reduce blood pressure. Thiamin plays a role in liver health!

*The Amaranth Family Benefits*

This family is made up of roots, seeds, greens, and herbs. Typically speaking they grow great in tougher climates that may have high altitudes, colder weather, or rough terrain. Beets fall into this family. And all of the members provide great Vitamin C which helps repair the body's muscle tissue, improve collagen, process iron, and much more.

## 11 LEAFY GREENS FROM SEED TO TABLE

This wouldn't be a vegetable book if we didn't include our leafy greens. Let's talk about how we can sow, grow, and harvest our favorites like artichoke, celery, and a few surprises.

## *Cardoon*

Despite being a perennial, cardoon is often grown as an annual. Being a member of the artichoke family, you want to have plenty of room for this guy. It can grow two feet wide and up to four feet tall with six hours of full sun and a nice lump of organic matter surrounding it. It grows best with a soil pH level of 6.0 to 7.0.

**How to Plant:**

1. Sow or transplant your seeds ¼ inch deep three to four weeks after the last (average) frost date in spring. The row should be set 36 to 48 inches apart.
2. In the beginning, you want to keep the soil moist until germination which typically occurs fourteen to thirty days at 75 degrees Fahrenheit.
3. Thin your cardoon 18 inches to 24 inches apart.
4. When it comes to watering the cardoon, let the plant dry out to one-inch soil before re-watering.
5. Cardoon will be ready to harvest after 120 days. Wear gloves so that you aren't pricked and dig down to slice the "celery-looking" stocks at the root to harvest.

## *Chicory*

Chicory is a cool-tolerant plant and loves to be put on salad. It's also a perennial but can be grown as an annual. You need an area with full sun because it does not tolerate any shade well. The soil also should be greater than a 5.5 in pH level.

**How to Plant:**

1. Seeds should be sown two to three weeks before the last frost date. Set them ¼ inch deep with 6 inches between seeds. Your rows actually need 2 feet of space
2. In order to thrive with this vegetable, you need to pay close attention to weeds and ensure the soil drains well.
3. You'll need to water the plants weekly with 1-2 inches of water to keep the soil moist.
4. Harvesting the root is the forced way and requires you to snap the plant at the root before the first frost and replant it in the sand.
5. Unforced growing is for those who want to use the plant for its leaves. It's recommended that you harvest while the leaves are still wound tight because the more it blooms the more bitter the leaves get.

## *Globe Artichoke*

Globe artichokes have these beautifully intriguing flower heads. You may also be surprised to learn how big they can get. In fact, they can grow to five feet tall. This crop does best when you start in early to mid-spring. Depending on where you grow, it can be an annual or a perennial. Interestingly enough it does best in sandy or loam sand type and while it likes full sun, it also works in partial shade. It's important to note that these guys are a long-term investment.

**How to Plant:**

1. When you plant in early to mid-spring you should know that you will not harvest until early summer of the next year.
2. Sow the seeds about ½ inch deep into the soil and space them 10 to 12 inches apart.
3. Continue to provide rich compost with potassium around the plant to nourish. They have deep roots so watering one to three times a week is important, especially in warmer climates.
4. From about June the next year you can harvest the buds when they are about the size of a golf ball. You may notice a secondary bud come up and this too can be harvested.

*Lettuce*

Lettuce is something we all love to grow because we can use it for salads or burgers. Consider this to be another cool-crop veggie that does fairly well in the fall and spring for most regions. For those who don't have patience, this is also a great crop as it grows quickly allowing staggered planting. Lettuce needs six hours of full sun each day.

**How to Plant:**

1. Sow into the soil two to four weeks before the last frost date about ⅛ to 1/4 inch into the soil. This will allow the seeds to germinate because of the light.
2. Plant or thin loose leaf lettuce to four inches apart to give them space. Romaine lettuce requires eight inches and iceberg requires 16 inches. Rows should have 12-15 inches of space.
3. Sow seeds every two weeks to have a staggered harvest and continuous crop.
4. In the beginning, water thoroughly with a mist nozzle. Overwatering can lead to disease growth and soggy plants.
5. You can remove the outer leaves before maturity to let the inner leaves continue to

grow. Otherwise, you can cut or dig up right around one inch above the soil line.

## Swiss Chard

Spinach is great but finding an alternative is sweet. That's why this delicious Swiss Chard is worth growing. It needs full sun and does best in well-nourished soil between 6.0 to 7.0 pH. Expect to give your veggies 1 to 1 ½ inches of water each week.

### How to Plant:

1. Sow your seeds in a sunny spot about ½ inch deep into the soil. Your rows should be spaced 15 inches apart to allow room for growth.
2. After the seeds grow, thin your chard to about 10 inches apart and continue to water thoroughly.
3. You'll notice that full leaves will appear around ten to twelve weeks, which is when you can harvest them. For continuous growth, cut off the outer leaves letting the rest grow and mature.

*Beets*

Beets surprise some people but if we think of them in their original form they have leafy greens, too. Beets will not do well in warm weather so it's best to plant them in the spring and fall. While shade-tolerant, they like to have more than four hours of sun a day.

**How to Plant:**

1. Start in early spring as soon as you can work with the soil.
2. Ensure that the soil selection you work with is free of rocks, roots, or other things that would disrupt root growth.
3. Sow the seeds ½ inch deep with spacing of 1 to 2 inches in between. Your rows should be spaced 12 to 18 inches apart.
4. Once greens get to be about 4 to 5 inches tall you will want to thin plants 3 to 4 inches apart. You can eat any of the greens you snip off.
5. Give 1 inch of water weekly to your beets while also continuing to mulch and nourish them.
6. After fifty-five to seventy days, the beets will likely reach maturity. To harvest, dig up the roots when beetroots are golf ball size or larger.

## *Quinoa*

Quinoa has grown very popular for its seeds but its leaves are also incredibly high in amino acids much like spinach. It is a part of the Amarnath family and is an annual. Quinoa needs full sun and, crazy enough, grows to be about four feet tall. It will grow best in pH soil levels of 6.0 to 7.5 that drains well and is loamy with nutritious compost!

**How to Plant:**

1. Sow seeds directly into soil that has been worked with compost right after the last frost date.
2. The seeds should be barely covered at all by the soil and spaced 10 to 12 inches apart in each row with a foot of space in between rows. Plant two to three seeds together so that at least one survives.
3. Spray the top of the soil to give it some moisture after planting. You can expect the seed to germinate after four to five days.
4. Maintenance will include continual weeding so the plant is not crowded while keeping the soil moist.
5. The seeds will be ready to harvest between 90 and 120 days. You'll have to bend over the seed

heads and clip them off. You'll want to spread your seeds over a screen and leave them out to dry.

## Corn

Corn is in everything whether we know it or not so it's only natural that we grow it ourselves! Technically speaking it's not a leafy green but since it's grown for its seeds, it's very similar to quinoa. Corn needs six to eight hours of full sun and is an annual. You'll need a long frost-free season to work with this vegetable.

**How to Plant:**

1. Direct sow seeds into the soil about two weeks after the last frost date and roughly 1 ½ to 2 inches into the ground. Space 4 to 6 inches apart with your rows having plenty of space 30 to 36 inches apart.
2. You can stagger start your planting by a few weeks to create multiple harvests to extend your season.
3. Water well after planting and at 3 to 4 inches tall thin your plants to 8 to 12 inches apart to allow room for growth. Continue to aim for two inches of water per week.

4. For plants that are tall and in windy conditions keep them straight up by mounting 12 inches of compost around the base.
5. Corn takes 60 to 100 days from seed to harvest but will show signs of maturity fifteen to twenty-three days after silking.

## Asparagus

While asparagus may be its own family, it's still considered to be a leafy green. Asparagus is wonderful on the grill which is why I am so happy to have this on the list. Because you'll only get the chance to sow this perennial in the spring, you want to plan accordingly. Some plants last up to fifteen years if planted right! Make sure they are in a spot where they can get eight full hours of sun per day. Keep in mind this is a long process and takes one to two years.

**How to Plant:**

1. Ensure your pH soil levels are between 6.5 and 7.0 as your asparagus will not tolerate acidic soils. It also needs to be well-draining.
2. Asparagus is usually grown from the crown but in this case, we will grow from the seed. Sow seeds 1 inch deep and 2 to 3 inches apart. Rows should be a foot apart.

3. It will take two to three weeks to germinate and when fall rolls around, you will want to cover them with hay to keep them warm throughout the fall.

4. A year later, once they are crowns, you can move them to a new location. Dig a trench 12 inches deep and 12 inches wide. Carefully taking the entire root plant with them in the weed-free trenches.

5. Water one inch per week to keep the soil moist. Once spears start to emerge in spring you may think it's time to harvest. Not yet. They should be harvested when they are six to eight inches and strong and healthy. Cut them with scissors or a sharp knife at ground level.

### Celery

Celery, in my opinion, is an underrated vegetable because you can do so much with it, despite so many people thinking it's boring! Celery is a biennial and as part of the Umbellifers family. Still a leafy green, though! Like asparagus, celery does best in six to eight hours of direct sun.

**How to Plant:**

1. Since celery is a cool-weather crop you'll either need to plant in middle to late spring or the middle of fall. However, it does not tolerate frost which makes timing a little tricky.
2. Since celery can take up to four-months you can start your seedlings indoors instead of trying to battle the weather.
3. The night before planting, you can soak your seed in warm water to help them germinate faster. Then you'll want to choose a place in your home in direct sunlight.
4. In a container put your seedlings on top of the soil and press lightly. You do not need to cover them. It's recommended to cover loosely with plastic wrap that can keep the seeds warm. You'll also want to consider using a grow light because they'll need sixteen hours of light once they are seedlings.
5. Once your seedlings are about two inches in height this is when they are ready to be transplanted outdoors. Sow the seedlings ½ inch deep into the soil with 8 inches of space in between.
6. Water regularly to keep the soil moist at all times.

7. When the stalks reach eight inches they are ready to be harvested. Use a knife to make a diagonal cut at the bottom of the stalk.

## LEAFY GREENS ARE SUPERHERO VEGETABLES

Leafy greens raise the bar slightly when it comes to challenging yourself with gardening. But the benefits are worth it as they are some of the most nutritious vegetables out there. Many love growing these veggies because they also happen to be low in calories, making it easy for those who are health conscious. With any of the leafy greens, you can extend the planting season by staggering your seeds as long as they meet the weather requirements. This allows for multiple harvests instead of a one-and-done meal.

# THE LEGUMES

If you are anything like me then you love variety when it comes to food. I am constantly searching my fridge for a good snack before dinner but that doesn't mean I am ready to give up any meals. This was my immediate draw to the legumes bunch. I wanted to feel like Ratatouille and throw the kitchen sink at my friends and family. Legumes are often loved by vegetarians for their high-protein benefit. Regardless of your diet preferences, they're great for everyone.

## HOW TO IDENTIFY A LEGUME

The legume family has 15,000 different species and is grown in climates all over the world. With that many, you may think it's impossible to identify what an actual legume is. But identifying legumes isn't that hard. Interestingly enough legumes have pods that contain seeds. Think snow peas or green beans! Officially they are called Fabaceae or referenced as Leguminosae, but for the purpose of not getting tongue-twisted, we can just call them legumes.

Legumes have a ton of health benefits which is why they are such an attractive vegetable to consider growing in the first place. For instance, they can lower your blood pressure and cholesterol while protecting against Diabetes Type II. For those who do have Diabetes, they can also help improve your glycemic and lipid controls. This is all because they are high in iron, calcium, potassium, magnesium, and antioxidants.

So, let's talk about ten very popular legumes that are worth gardening. Warning: if you don't like beans, you may need to skip this chapter. However, if you have a pre-conceived notion of beans; let me change your mind!

*Hint: There is a surprise at the end!*

### Chickpeas

Chickpeas are a tasty protein that can be used for so many great things. Hummus, salads, a snack and so much more. But chickpeas are fragile and don't tolerate cold or extremely hot weather well. They have a long growing season so precision with when to plant is important. Where is also important as they need six to eight hours of sun a day. It is an annual legume, meaning you'll have to replant each year.

**How to Plant:**

1. It's not a bad idea to sow the seed indoors in little pots. You can sow them 1 to 2 inches deep. If you want to sow into the ground do it 1 to 2 weeks before the last frost and insulate them with a covering.
2. Use a biodegradable pot as they don't transplant well and you will want to just put it

directly in the ground. You can also fit up to two seeds one to two inches apart in the pot. You can expect sprouting in about two weeks.

3. In mild temperatures, water gently once a day. Hotter temperatures will require twice a day.

4. When the plants are 3 to 4 inches you can transplant them in an area that gets six hours of full sun. You also want to avoid nitrogen-rich soil because it will decrease your yield. Adding aged compost a week before can help significantly.

5. Transplant your pots into the ground completely and space 4 to 5 inches apart. Rows should be 18 to 24 inches apart. Continue to mulch to maintain soil moisture as it gets warmer.

6. Harvest the entire plant once the pods have turned brown. Some like to just snap off the pods when they are green and fresh which is OK, too!

### Peas

I can always remember my mom reminding me to eat my peas as a kid. I never wanted to. But now I am growing them! Peas are also annuals but need just four to five hours of sun per day. The entire growing season is sixty to seventy days. Make sure the ground has warmed up a little bit in the spring before planting.

**How to Plant:**

1. Make trenches about two inches deep and sow seeds two to three inches apart in space. You can plant in single rows or double rows. Cover them and water.
2. Sometimes peas will need some support so using mesh wiring to help them is always a good idea. You'll also need to control pests and do a lot of weeding to support them.
3. To ensure water is enough, stick your finger about 2 inches deep in the soil. If it's dry, water!
4. Since peas are easy, you can harvest when the pods are firm and about three inches. Simply pick them off!

*Kidney Beans*

I love kidney beans in my chili. Remember that they must always be dried and then cooked because of their toxicity. Kidney beans are also perennials that grow back year after year. They need six to eight hours of full sun and need well-draining soil. They do best in warmer temperatures.

**How to Plant:**

1. Sow seeds after the last frost 1 ½ inches below the soil with four inches of space in between. Some varieties need eight inches. You can expect seedlings between ten to fourteen days.
2. Sowing two seeds together gives you a better chance. You can always thin the weaker one out.
3. Because kidney beans produce their own nitrogen you don't have to worry as much about the soil. They are a low maintenance crop. Only water to keep the soil moist, not wet. Keep in mind if you are growing a pole variety, it will need some support as it gets larger.
4. You can harvest between 100 and 140 days which makes them a long-term crop. They are ready when the beans are plump. Remove the entire plant from the ground and hang it upside down to dry.

*Pinto Beans*

Moving onto Mexican food brings us to pinto beans. Unlike kidneys, pinto beans are annuals. They need six hours of sunlight a day throughout the summer for optimal growth. They also have pole and bush varieties like kidneys and are incredibly easy to care for and grow.

**How to Plant:**

1. In composted soil sow your seeds 1 ½ inches below soil level with 4 to 6 inches of space between seeds and 2 feet between the rows. For bush varieties give move space and for pole varieties provide support.
2. After this, you will only need to water when the soil has dried out. Do not overwater because they can't withstand wet roots.
3. After 90-150 days, they will be ready for harvesting. Pull the entire plant and hang it to dry out.

## *Lentils*

It's no exaggeration when I say lentils are some of the most nutrient-dense foods you can eat. Between the fiber and protein, these annuals have a lot to offer. Be prepared for a long growing season as these guys won't be ready to harvest until 80 to 110 days while needing six to eight hours of sun per day.

**How to Plant:**

1. Plant your seeds about two weeks before the last frost date as lentils grow best during hot summers.
2. Sow your seeds one inch deep with 18 inches of space between rows. You'll need to thin your seedlings to five inches apart as lentils need space. You also need to inoculate seeds with rhizobacteria so the roots can absorb nitrogen.
3. Consider giving these guys at least an inch of water in well-draining soil per week. If the plants get too hot it can minimize the crop yield.
4. Continue to fertilize with high-nitrogen compost by adding mulch to the area. While doing this, keep an eye out for pests and diseases.
5. As you approach harvesting, stop water to let the seeds and vines dry out. Once dry, take the whole vine and pluck the pods. Remove the seeds from the pods and spread them out on a tray to dry out.

*Tip: Add your vines back to your compost!*

### *Green Bush Beans*

Green beans, as we are learning, can be grown in two ways. By pole or by bush. It's worth talking about each one individually because they do differ. Green bush beans are called tender annuals and work in compact spaces so if you have to grow out of a container this works. They need a lot of sun so find a nice spot that gets six to eight hours a day. You should also note that there are a few varieties to choose from.

**How to Plant:**

1. Start by preparing your garden with organic mulch that is well-draining. And remember it needs to be very sunny! This is true even if you grow them in containers.
2. You want to sow your seeds about an inch deep with three inches of space between your seeds. If there are multiple rows, you need to ensure about 18 inches of space in between them.
3. Definitely water immediately after you plant your seeds. Eventually, you will see true leaves pop up. Once you see two of them, thin your green beans to about six inches in space between the plants.
4. After routinely watering, managing pests, and weeding, keep in mind that you don't need to

add nitrogen because green beans have enough of their own. Too much is no good.

5. After forty to sixty days, you can pick out your best beans. Look for long and crisp beans with sturdy pods on the inside. Pick the pods right off the plant as soon as they are ready. Waiting too long can change the texture of the pods.

### Green Pole Beans

Now let's talk about green pole beans. You still get the delicious green beans mentioned above but you need to grow them slightly differently. These guys grow vertically on vines and need support. These are great for gardens that don't have a lot of space. These will take six to eight weeks to harvest. They also need about eight hours of full sun and are annuals.

**How to Plant:**

1. You will want to sow your seeds 4 to 8 inches apart in rows with plenty of space. The rows need 24 to 36 inches of space. They will do best about 1 inch below the soil surface level. You will need plant support for the vines to wrap around. (At least 6 feet high)
2. Understand that pole beans need at least one inch of water per week immediately after

planting. You also need to pay close attention to the disease and pest control.

3. Once they start to bloom, you need to help them get on the support by helping wrap the vine around in the beginning. Once you do this, they will naturally do it on their own.

4. To harvest, you want to pick them when ready just like you would with the bush varieties. Avoid old beans that become woody and focus on getting the pods every three to five days.

### Lima beans

Another bean that seriously packs a punch. Lima beans are native to Central America but do well anywhere that offers a warm climate. Joining their friends as a tender annual, they are rich in iron, protein, thiamine, and riboflavin. They need no less than eight hours of direct sunlight for optimal growth.

**How to Plant:**

1. Sow your lima bean seeds about three to four weeks after the average last frost date. They do best sown 1 to 1 ½ inches deep into the soil. Your seeds should be 2 to 4 inches apart and the rows need to have 2 feet in space.

2. Thin your seedlings 4 to 6 inches apart after they germinate. You also will want to water 1 inch per week to keep promoting healthy plant growth.

3. Lima beans are easy to plant and will be ready to harvest eighty-five to ninety days after sowing the seeds. This is a long, hot growing season. Once they are visibly plump, pick the pods off the plant.

### Peanuts

What? We love peanuts. Surprise! This can be grown and classified as a pea. This is a warm-weather perennial and has one of the longer growing seasons. In fact, they won't be ready to harvest until 120-130 days. None of these days can have any frost! This means you need to be really selective when you start to grow these legumes. Surprisingly these plants can grow from 6 to 30 inches tall depending on the variety. So plan accordingly.

### How to Plant:

1. When soil reaches 65 degrees Fahrenheit (usually three to four weeks after the last frost) you can finally sow your seeds into the soil. Sow 1 ½ inches to 3 inches into the ground.

They need 6 to 8 inches of space and give about 18 inches of space between rows.

2. Once your plants reach 12 inches in height, mound your compost and soil around the base to provide support.

3. Water around one inch per week evenly around the plant. Manage any rodent control until the leaves turn yellow. When this happens it's an indicator that they are ready to harvest. Dig up the roots, shaking off any clinging soil and take the pods off. Now you can unshell them!

Legume pulses are incredibly easy to store. And while we will get into the storage of your vegetables and hard work later, it's worth noting this as it's one of the benefits. There is nothing worse than spending a lot of time and dedication on a vegetable that goes bad within a few days of harvesting it. This won't be the case with legumes if cared for properly. This way you can have your legumes year-round regardless of most of them needing a hot warm season.

7

# THE NIGHTSHADES

The nightshades are a great group of vegetables to work with because they are a lot of staples in recipes. For instance, tomatoes and potatoes can be used in a variety of recipes in nearly every food culture. Now, of course, some could debate that the tomatoes or some of the nightshades are actually a fruit. Rather than focus on that, let's remain focused on gardening and how to get these nightshades plump and tasty for a great harvest.

## WHAT FOODS FALL INTO THE NIGHTSHADES FAMILY?

Alkaloids are the main characteristic that determines whether these fruits or vegetables are considered to be in the nightshade group. Alkaloids are specific kinds of chemicals that can be found in certain plants. These specific chemicals include nitrogen and essentially would need to have an impact on the human body from a medicinal standpoint. The two most common examples we are familiar with are morphine and quinine. They come from plants.

Now that doesn't mean that when we are growing these vegetables that we are suddenly making medicinal drugs. Tobacco is another nightshade that contains alkaloids. This brings us to the conclusion that some nightshades can be good for your health while others have a negative impact.

So let's talk about the nightshades that we want to grow and harvest. There are definitely a few favorites of mine on this list.

## *Potatoes*

Potato soup, baked potato, casseroles. Whatever you love to use potatoes for, it's such a great vegetable to learn how to garden. There are hundreds of thousands of recipes out there that call for potatoes. These annuals do best in acidic soil that is between pH 5.0-5.5 with a lot of rainfall. For those who live in the north, you will likely try to plant these guys in the summer whereas the south is looking more at wintertime. Regardless, potatoes need six full hours of sun per day so a sunny spot is mandatory.

**How to Plant:**

1. When there is no more frost and the soil is easily workable is when you can think about sowing your seeds into the ground. Remember to check for the right acid levels and ensure the soil is loosened rather than packed down. It needs to drain well.

2. Right before you plant, you can cut a large potato into golf ball sized pieces with one to three "eyes" or indentations into the potato. If a seed potato is no bigger than an egg, plant it whole.

3. Space your rows about three feet apart with trenches that are about 6 inches wide and 8

inches deep for the potatoes to be sewn into the soil. Place your seed potato cut face down into the ground with 12 to 14 inches of space in between the potato seeds. Cover with 3 to 4 inches of soil.

4. Sprouts will appear about twelve to sixteen days later. This is when you can cover the trenches with the rest of the soil. This is roughly three more inches to full cover. As potatoes grow through the soil, keep mounding the soil as they do better in darkness.

5. Water 1 to 2 inches a week to retain moisture within the soil but also make sure it's not soggy. If your potatoes become exposed to the sun they can turn green and produce a toxic chemical. Keep this in mind.

6. Different varieties will have different harvesting dates. Regardless, be careful pulling up roots and working not to puncture or bruise the potato. Typically, this is two to three weeks after the foliage has died down. You can cut it back and about two weeks later dig up your potatoes.

## *Tomatoes*

Tomatoes are one of the best nightshades because I use them every day in all my recipes. Now, there are a lot of different tomatoes out there from roma tomatoes to cherry tomatoes. Here we are going to talk about working with cherry tomatoes. Technically speaking, tomatoes are perennials but they are often grown as annuals. They need six to eight hours of sunlight to thrive so make sure they get put in a good spot! They also have a very specific soil pH level with 6.2 to 6.5 being the goal.

**How to Plant:**

1. Seedlings that are 6 to 10 inches tall are ready to be planted into the soil. Regardless of whether you started your seedlings indoors or purchased them, you need to be sure there is no more frost. Since they grow to be big and bushy, leave a lot of space (a few feet) in between planting holes.
2. Plant your stalk in the soil after trimming some of the shoots from the bottom of the main stem. You can pick them all the way up to the soil line and leave the rest. Using compost and lime to surround the stalk will help nourish it.

3. Where branches meet the stalk and form a V are called suckers. Continue to pinch these off so the plant can focus on making the fruit (tomato). Water heavily once a week rather than evenly throughout the week.

4. Cherry tomatoes will be ready to pick after a few months. They are going to be best to pick when they start to turn their expected color. But don't wait too long!

## *Eggplants*

Eggplants are warm-weather friends that are picked best when they are just reaching their maturity. Just like your tomatoes, be prepared for these plants to grow very tall (a few feet in height). Depending on where you live you may need to start indoors about two months before actually transplanting in order to avoid the frost. They are perennials but more commonly grown as annuals and, like the other members of the family, rely on six hours of sunlight a day. Something that throws people off is that eggplants can turn out to be a variety of colors and not just purple. They can be pink, white, green, black, etc.

**How to Plant:**

1. If you are starting indoors you will need to use a five-gallon container that will absorb sunlight well. A five-gallon container can host one plant. Sow your seed ¼ inch deep into the soil.
2. After the last frost you can plant your seedlings in holes that are spaced 24 to 30 inches apart. Your rows should also be spaced about 3 feet apart from each other. Eggplants need plenty of space to grow.
3. Right after you plant you should set up stakes that are 24 inches high and spaced 1-2 inches from the plant. This will provide the needed support as they grow. Also, water well so that soil is moist 6 inches deep.
4. After this, you can add a new layer of mulch/compost to nourish the plant. For any plants that start to get big, only allow five to six fruits while pinching off any other buds so it doesn't get overcrowded.
5. From seed, eggplants will take 100 to 120 days to harvest. Don't pull your fruit off, you need to cut with a knife because you can end up damaging it. You will know when they are ripe when you press on the skin and it is softer.

## *Peppers*

Peppers are great for a number of recipes and are very similar to the rest of the family. They are warm-weather nightshades and need to be completely free of frost. The best soil pH level to garden peppers is in between 6.0-7.0. You will also want to make sure that they find a nice sunny home as they need six hours of direct sunlight a day. Regardless of the type of peppers (shishito, bell, sweet) you are working with, they are all considered to be perennials but typically grown as annuals. Under the right conditions you can expect them to come back again and again.

**How to Plant:**

1. Sow your seedlings 1 inch deep and 18 to 24 inches apart in a well-drained area with plenty of sunlight. Right after sowing, mix your organic matter in, to nourish the pepper seedlings.
2. Water immediately and provide 1-2 inches of water per week evenly. You'll also need to provide some sort of support for the fruit to not weigh down the stems.
3. These are relatively easy fruits to deal with as you just need to continue to water and add compost to nourish. Expect yields to come

around sixty-ninety days. Because you can't tug
on the branches out of fear of breaking them,
use a sharp knife to cut the pepper off.

## Chilis

While chili's are technically a part of the pepper family,
it is worth giving them their own section. But we can
come back to the idea that all peppers are perennials
but typically grown as annuals. They need six hours of
full sun just like the entire pepper family. What makes
them slightly different is they have an incredibly
variant harvesting season from 60 to 150 days because
of a number of factors. Your seed packet will indicate a
better range for you.

**How to Plant:**

1. You may want to start by sowing your seeds in
   a greenhouse or in small pots by a sunny
   window. Starting in January, because of how
   long their growing season lasts, is not a bad
   idea. You can sow the seed right on the top of
   the soil and sprinkle a little more compost
   lightly over them.
2. Germination will only take seven to ten days. In
   the meantime and afterward, you want to keep
   the soil moist at all times without making it wet

or soggy. You will want to water sparingly, keeping it a little drier than most vegetables or fruits.

3. When seedlings are strong enough to transplant, you can either plant them directly into the ground in a sunny area or transfer them to grow bags to grow individually.

4. Once you get your first flowering shoot you actually want to pinch that off to get more shoots to grow. Starting in July you can likely start picking the chili peppers. What is interesting about this fruit is that the more you pick the more chilis will grow. Use a knife to slice them off.

### *Tomatillos*

If this is the first time you are being introduced to a tomatillo then you have an exciting journey ahead of you. It's not a tomato but has similar properties. It's green and slightly more acidic and resembles a pepper that looks like a tomato. It is often used in Mexican foods and salsas. Interestingly enough, in hardiness zones from five to nine they are annuals but in zones nine and ten they are considered perennials. Count on these nightshades needing six hours of sunlight a day just like the rest of the gang.

**How to Plant:**

1. Start them indoors six to eight weeks before the last frost date. You will want to sow them in groups of two to ensure one of the fruits works out. This is because it's not a self-pollinating plant. Your soil level needs to be around 7.0.
2. If you start them outdoors you will want to plant them ¼ inch deep with tons of spacing. Seedlings that are transplanted need to be 18-24 inches apart and your rows should be 3 to 4 feet in space. (You can also grow individually in five-gallon buckets or pots.)
3. They need frequent watering along with their sunny conditions. In this case they need the same treatment as tomatoes. Adding some more compost can also help control weeds. Also, beware of pests.
4. To harvest your tomatillos you can snip them from the root or stem. You can also pinch them with your fingers. You will know it's time to harvest when the husk on the outside starts to split.

There is nothing more frustrating than running down to the grocery store to buy a chili powder for your homemade chili only to find out it's super expensive.

When you grow peppers and chillies, the best part is that you can dry them out and make your own spices. No more spending $5 for a tiny jar that gets shoved in the back of the cabinet. But, of course, you don't have to dry your peppers out. They are great fresh as well.

Chilis, peppers, and all of the nightshades have a number of incredible benefits. They have a lot of fiber and vitamins packed inside them especially potassium in potatoes which helps muscle function properly. It also helps recover overly worked out muscles. Another reason why you should be growing and eating your veggies!

# 8

# DIGGING DOWN FOR THOSE ROOT VEGETABLES

R oot vegetables are the type of gardening that most of us imagine when we first start. Shaking the dirt off and pulling up a turnip is the ultimate sign of success! But with root vegetables, there are some different techniques used when it comes to gardening. For instance, you will see that using grow bags in this chapter can be particularly useful and make the process a lot easier. We are going to have some cross-over with some other vegetables from the previous chapters. This is because vegetables can be in more than one classification!

For instance, potatoes happen to be a root vegetable but are also in the nightshade family. Just like radishes are in the brassica family but also a root vegetable. In an effort to simplify things we talk about them in some of the previous chapters. Now we can use our knowledge to approach some vegetables differently.

## WHY WE LOVE ROOT VEGETABLES

Root vegetables are considered to be the fruits of the earth. We don't see them but they are nourished below to make tasty and healthy foods later on. The roots gather all the nutrients from the soil making them hearty while also offering some of the best health benefits to us. Typically, they come around in the fall time which is why we see them in a lot of thick dishes like stews, soups, and bisques. Let's dive into some of the overarching health benefits from these starchy vegetables.

Folate (Vitamin B-9) comes up again and again because it impacts healthy red blood cells. It's often given to pregnant women to boost their immune system. This goes right along with complex carbohydrates, potassium, and fiber. These are all staples to a healthy human diet. But we also get a fair share of other vitamins from root vegetables like carrots. Carrots provide a lot of Vitamin A which also supports a strong and healthy immune system. Of course, the best part is that they are low in calories and fat for the most part!

## NINE VEGETABLES TO ROOT FOR!

So now that we know root vegetables are the bomb, let's make sure we talk about the most common ones to the garden. It's also worth understanding why each individual root vegetable has something to offer. Let's get into it.

### Carrots

Finally, the vegetable everyone has been waiting for. Carrots are one of the most popular vegetables that come to mind, let alone it being a popular root vegetable. The best thing about carrots is they are an easy vegetable to grow and give you a lot of bang for your buck. In other words, you get a great crop.

You'll grow this as an annual likely but it is considered to be a biennial. Interestingly enough, carrots are one of few vegetables that like sandy soil so make sure it's free draining. We also need to place them in a spot with plenty of sun as they require six to ten hours of sun. The great news is: baby carrots can be harvested in thirty days while larger ones take about fifty to eighty days.

**How to Plant:**

1. Carrots should be sown about two to three weeks before the average last frost date. Or you can sow in late summer going into the fall when things start to cool off but well before the fall frost.

2. Sow your seeds about ¼ inch into the soil with 1 to 2 inches of space between seedlings and 1 or 2 feet of space between rows. You want to add several inches of compost over them to bury them well. Your compost should have wood ashes to help with the fertility of the soil so it's between 5.5 and 6.8 pH.

3. Ideally, if you are struggling with rocks and other things in your soil, you can always plant in raised beds or soil mounds for an easier time.

4. Evenly water carrots keeping the soil moist but not soaking. As your carrots begin to reach maturity you can cut back on your watering. When your carrots reach 2 inches tall, thin

them out to 2 inches apart. Snip the plants off at the crown.

5. Next, halfway through your full season, pick up some baby carrots leaving equal amounts of space between your other carrots to provide room to grow. Fill any open spaces with compost or mulch.

6. To harvest, you can lift the carrots where the soil is loose. If packed, loosen the soil first so you don't ruin your crop.

### *Ginger*

Ginger is a powerful and flavorful root vegetable (herb) that really gets our sinuses going. We love it because of its anti-inflammatory benefits. In fact, it's so strong many people use it for arthritis. It's grown as an annual and needs about two to five hours of sunlight per day. It's a warm-weather crop that loves organically rich and loamy soil.

### How to Plant:

1. First, you need to cut ginger rhizomes into 1 or 1 ½ pieces. Then they need a few days to heal after being cut. Then on a good early day in spring, you can plant the ones that are plump and have a few buds.

2. Plant your rhizomes 2 to 4 inches deep with 6 to 8 inches of space between each one. Your growth buds should be pointing upwards when planted. Note that your ginger plants grow to be about 2 to 3 feet tall.

3. You will always want to keep the plants from drying out. But overwater is dangerous so using a sprayer or mister is the key here. As the weather cools, you will need less and less.

4. After eight to ten months of watering and adding compost when necessary, ginger can be harvested. You can take the entire plant up by the root. Then you can start the process again by choosing certain rhizomes for replanting.

### Turmeric

Introducing Curcuma Longa. What? Indian saffron is another name for turmeric that is given because of its common use in India. There are so many benefits to consuming turmeric but it also plays a role in ayurvedic medicine. The most notable benefits are heart health, preventing Alzheimer's and cancer, as well as being an antioxidant which makes this root vegetable worth the 200-300 day harvest. Typically, this is nine to ten months.

**How to Plant:**

1. Start indoors about eight to ten weeks prior to the last average frost date since they have a long growing season. Lay individual "fingers" horizontally in a seed tray. If they have already sprouted, they need to face upwards.
2. Once it gets warmer you will want to work the soil 8 to 12 inches and make sure it's nice and crumbly with a lot of ability for drainage. Add compost to enrich the soil. Plant 4 inches deep and 3 feet apart without mounding or hilling the soil. Just cover.
3. Once planted into the garden, water the sprouts with 1 inch of water per week. Continue to keep an eye out for pests and weeds weekly as turmeric plants have strong scents that attract them.
4. After starting indoors, fall time will be when you can harvest these big plants. To do so use a garden fork to loosen the soil around the plant. Once loosened you can dig up the entire thing. You can cut off all the foliage at the crown and discard it. The rest is your fresh turmeric!

*Onions*

Onions have a wide variety of colors, shapes, and sizes. Some of them are biennials while others are perennials. Almost all of them, however, are grown as annuals. All bubs will need at least twelve hours of sun while some varieties need even thirteen to sixteen hours. They also have a long growing season and won't be ready to harvest until three to four months. Some varieties may not show a bulb till their second season.

**How to Plant:**

1. Onions can be started from seeds, seedlings, or even bulbs. In this case, let's start with seeds. Start them six to eight weeks indoors before the last frost date. You want to bury them ¼ inch deep in the soil. Expect germination in four to ten days. Thin your seedlings 1 to 2 inches and rows 12 to 18 inches apart.
2. As the last frost date approaches, get ready to transplant outdoors. When the ground is workable make 4-inch deep furrows and space your seedlings 6 inches apart. Make sure the soil is weed-free. Well-draining soil can prevent diseases like fungi among others.
3. Water about one inch once a week rather than evenly daily. To retain the moisture you can lay

down 8 to 10 inches of compost. This is better than overwatering which can cause the onions to split.

4. When the leaves start to turn yellow and droop, the soil can dry out some. Once the bulbs pop out the stalks will begin to droop. Once the top half of the bulbs have fallen over, you can pull the rest of them to harvest. Cut the bulbs 1 ½ inches from the stalk to harvest.

## *Garlic*

Garlic is a great staple flavor to a lot of fantastic dishes. When it comes to gardening there are two varieties: soft neck and hard neck garlic. It's often grown as an annual either way and will thrive in six to eight hours of direct sun. Regardless, consider buying your planting garlic from local stores as garlic can be temperamental to the area it is grown in.

**How to Plant:**

1. Garlic does best in chilly weather which is why you should plant in the fall or early spring. Your soil needs to be loose and fertile with well-draining capabilities. Include a generous heaping of organic matter for nutrition. Ensure it's in neutral soil between 6.0 and 7.0.

2. Place pulled apart cloves without the paper shell 1 to 2 inches into the soil. The ridges of the clove should face upwards. Add 4 to 6 inches of compost on top. Water ½ to 1 inch every week.

3. By early spring (if planted in the fall) you will notice the garlic start to pop up. Remove the mulch away from the leaves. Once they hit 6 inches tall you can add more mulch around them for nutrition. Once leaves turn yellow slow watering to allow them to harden.

4. Expect garlic to be ready anywhere from July to September. The stems will turn yellow and fall over while the leaves will turn brown. To harvest, carefully dig at the root keeping stems intact. Cut the stems 1 1/2 inches from the bulb to harvest.

### Parsnips

My mother's Sanday roast is why I was drawn to growing my own parsnips. It's also one of the most simple root vegetables to grow which makes it that more attractive. They are biennials that need a nice sunny space to do well. They take up a lot of space so expect to space them 1 to 3 feet tall and 6 to 12 inches wide.

**How to Plant:**

1. When using fresh parsnip seeds between April to June in the springtime, the soil needs to be weed and rock free allowing the roots to grow without disruption. Sow the seed ½ to 1 inch deep with 12 to 18 inches in space. Don't be surprised at slow germination as it takes up to twenty-eight days.
2. When they start to get larger in size thin to about 3 inches. Since they are such an easy plant to care for, you only need to water occasionally to keep the soil moist. Weed occasionally between rows.
3. Late fall is when you will find these root vegetables ready to harvest. Simply dig around the roots loosening the soil. That's it! Simple!

### Sweet Potato

Sweet potatoes happen to be one of my absolute favorite vegetables. It's a healthy carb that can also be turned into a sweet dessert. It is a warm-season vegetable grown in the U.S and needs six hours of sun to do well. Something funny is that sweet potatoes are not related to regular potatoes. They have similar properties, though, and need to be planted in the spring to have four warm weather months to grow correctly. Even though they are technically perennial, they are grown as annuals in acidic soil between 5 to 6.5.

**How to Plant:**

1. Slips will need to be planted 12 to 18 inches apart and with plenty of space between the rows–3 to 4 feet is usually enough space. This is because of the vines filling in.
2. The soil needs to be well-draining and high in organic matter and compost. Keep in mind that there needs to be an acidic pH level.
   Interestingly enough, sandier soil works best.
3. Since these vegetables do better in dry soil, you can see that they only need one inch of water per week in an evenly distributed fashion.
4. About three to four months later you will notice that the tubers will be ready. Look for the leaves to start to turn yellow as an indicator that they are ready to harvest.

*Yam*

Yam is easily mistaken for sweet potatoes which is why we wanted to put it up next on our list. Yams are planted as annuals and can be harvested after one season. They love to have about six hours of full sunlight and their soil must be prepared well. But what most people don't know is that yams grow huge in tubers that can be six feet tall! Having said that, they don't require too much attention after planting. Hardiness zones 8 to 10 will do the best with growing yams and need slightly acidic soil from 5.5 to 6.5 pH.

**How to Plant:**

1. Cut a yam tuber in quarters and ensure that it has one eye to grow a plant from. To prevent disease you can rub wood ash over them and allow them to sit for a few days.
2. They don't transplant well so sow directly into the ground about ¼ inch deep into the soil. Space 12 inches apart and give 3 feet in row space.
3. Give your tubers at least 12 inches of spacing between each other and more importantly ensure that your rows outside have 5 feet of space. After planting, you can water every day for the first week but then cut in half by the second week.
4. Every three weeks you can add organic matter low in nitrogen to keep nourishing the yams. You will see that the plant will grow to a few feet high not long after and can slow down the feeding.

5. If you want a companion plant, ensure that they are not spacious plants. Things like herbs will do well because they are tiny. Meanwhile, the only maintenance you need to keep an eye out for is pests and dry rot!

6. Yams will be in the ground for about eight months through your early spring, summer, and fall. Ensure harvesting them before winter or they'll die. Leaves will begin to yellow indicating you've got a few weeks left. To harvest, dig at the base to lift the full tubers out of the soil.

### Fennel

Fennel is something you probably haven't heard as much about before. It looks like some sort of combination between cabbage and dill. Both the bulb and fronds can be used. The fronds are usually great for a salad while the bulb has a licorice taste and can be grilled or sauteed. While it is a perennial it is grown as an annual. Count on giving this vegetable six hours of direct sun to do well. Also, note that they should not be companion planted with others!

**How to Plant:**

1. Plant fennel seeds 10-12 inches apart and about ⅛ inches deep.
2. Start by watering with a spray bottle. Once the shoots begin to appear, water frequently as you don't want the bulbs to dry out. As it continues to grow, consider stalking it once it reaches 18 inches tall. This is because some fennel plants can grow to 4 feet tall. Hill around the bulb to protect it from the sun.
3. After ninety days of caring for the fennel and ensuring no pests or diseases creep in, you can get ready to harvest. You can take a few leaves as soon as the plant is well established. Once the bulb is about the size of a tennis ball, you can cut the fronds from its base to harvest.

*BONUS TIP: Soak fennel seeds in water for two days for faster germination. Once the shoots begin to appear, transfer them into the container or ground.*

GETTING RIGHT TO THE ROOTS

Root vegetables are such a great sector of the entire vegetable group. They are awesome for fall dishes and provide us with a lot of daily nutrients to keep us energized and satisfied. The most important thing to keep in mind when it comes to root vegetables is that they need great soil to thrive in. Ensuring that the roots stay protected means clearing and working with your soil base beforehand. This just means getting rid of rocks, working the soil so it isn't hard and clumpy, and weeding the area.

This is how your root vegetables will be able to thrive. Any competition for their roots to grow in space can create a lot of problems. Also, remember that root vegetables usually have a few different uses. With many, their leaves can be harvested right along with the base of the vegetable. This is another great way to be green and environmentally friendly.

# 9

## TAKING ADVANTAGE OF THE VINE FAMILY

We've already come across a few favorites from the vine family such as tomatoes and some beans. And we are still learning that there are so many cross-sections when it comes to vegetables belonging to more than one family. The vine family can play a part in garden design which is aesthetically pleasing. Not only do I get satisfaction out of picking my vegetables but seeing the garden as a whole is a calming oasis. You can have that, too.

### WHAT IS A VINE PLANT?

Vines look beautiful as long as they have support. A vine plant has thin stem structures that are not made of wood and will use anything around it to find support to keep growing upwards and outwards. They can grow both vertically and often horizontally. Remarkably, their vine strength is incredibly strong, despite not being able to support themselves to grow upwards alone. But something to remember is that just because it looks like a duck and quacks like a duck, doesn't mean it is a duck in this case. Some plants look like vine plants but indeed are not.

So in order to have these beautiful plants in our garden, we need to have a trellis to support them. Here we can learn how to make a trellis or find an affordable option to have in our green gardens.

## HOW TO MAKE A TRELLIS?

First of all, what really is a trellis? A trellis is a structure that can be large or small that will help any climbing or growing plants in the vine family find support. In all the previously mentioned vegetables we talk about having different support for plants. A trellis is a great solution for all of this. Here we can talk about how to make it from different products at a low cost. While a trellis can stand on its own, one hack I like to keep in mind is adding one to a privacy fence if you have one. This spruces up the fence in general and is a functional idea!

### Bamboo Trellis

Bamboo can look great in a garden which is why this is one of my personal favorites. Order three bamboo sticks online or at a local garden center. Make sure that they are a few feet high. Now all you need is some twine to keep the bamboo sticks together but also to give the vines some support.

To make it, put your three bamboo shoots into the ground like stakes. They should be placed in a way that makes a triangle shape or if leaning against a fence in a row. Though, the triangular shape is easier to wrap the twine around. Voila, that's it!

### Repurposed Garden Tools

Just like your bamboo shoots you can use repurposed garden tools to create a cute-looking trellis. It goes with your garden theme so using shovels, rakes with smaller heads, and other tools that are similar in height can be a go-to. However, they need to be wood. Consider carving the bottom of your tools into stakes so they stick into the ground and you don't have to worry about them falling over.

You will also need some flat wood and nails. Nail the three garden tools together in three separate places at the bottom, middle, and top, with your flat wood. This will provide support for the vines to grow around.

### Coat Rack

Movable coat racks have to be one of the easiest ones because it's a household item we all have. You can also combine this with coat hangers to manipulate the twine easily to customize it to your plant's needs. The best part of this is you can paint it any color you want to make it a great design piece to your garden as well.

You may need to break down some of the coat rack to reglue them together in a way that works as a trellis. By understanding the basic shape of a trellis you can easily work the material to create a beautiful geometric design that is also functional.

### Cattle Panels

Cattle panels are something you probably don't come across as much unless you are a full-blown farmer. But even farmers can have gardens that are more casual.

They still need to use basic things like a trellis so finding things like cattle panels can be a great solution. Bring two cattle panels together to allow your vegetables to grow vertically. You can train a number of vegetables to do so and that makes saving space a lot easier.

### Window Frames

If you are a fan of rustic farmhouse decor then reusing window frames is right up your alley. While you will have to be very careful, poking out the glass of a wooden window frame can make an excellent trellis. It is such a unique piece to add to your garden that also can blend seamlessly. You also want to be careful of splinters and cracking wood frames.

You should bring some sort of chicken wire or twine that is strong enough to stand on its own to work into the frame. This will allow for the vines to wrap themselves around it and find the additional support it needs to grow vertically.

### Ladder

A big metal ladder is probably not going to do it. But a small structure that resembles a ladder would be a great way to make your own trellis. For this idea, the structure needs to be thin enough that the vines can wind around. Think step ladders or ladders with only three rungs. But for bigger vines that we see grow all up along the side of a house, you could use a massive ladder. Styling this is a tiny bit harder.

### Crib Railing

A crib railing is a perfect structure to make a trellis. This is all about sustainability and reusing products in a recyclable manner. When you use the side of the crib you don't need to do much as everything is really set in place. The railing is perfect for the vines and there is a lot of space for them to grow and options to wrap around different rungs.

## MORE VINE PLANTS WE CAN'T FORGET!

There are some other vine plants that we love to plant and garden. Whether it be caring for pumpkins for Halloween, enjoying summer squash, or any of the other vine plants that are worth taking the time to garden. They are all worth this list and something I highly recommend giving a try!

## *Pumpkin*

Give us a call, Charlie Brown, because we are going to find the perfect pumpkin for you. Pumpkins are great for pies and their seeds which is why this makes our list. This warm-season vegetable is a tender one so ensuring it gets what it needs is crucial. These vegetables are annuals that require one inch of water per week. If there is any chance of frost it could stunt or stop the growth of your pumpkin. Ensure it's passed. This means planting in early May or June.

**How to Plant:**

1. Pumpkins require a lot of space. In fact, you need 50 to 100 square feet per hill. You can plant your seed one inch deep and four to five per hill. You will also need 5 to 6 feet in space between hills. Your rows will need 10 to 15 inches.
2. You will need to use a hoe to continually weed. You also need to ensure that the soil has great irrigation so you can water through drier periods. This maintenance is on repeat until you get ready to harvest.
3. When you notice that pumpkins have turned a deep orange they are ready to harvest. This should fall around late September and mid-

144 | NOOR FATIMA

October. They should mature between 85-120 days. To harvest, cut the vine 3 to 4 inches with the stem attached. Using a sharp knife is best to make a clean cut.

## Cucumber

Cucumber is one of the most common vegetables when it comes to salads. Most people don't realize they are a vine plant. That's because they can also be grown as a bush variety. For this instance, we can focus on vine growing. They are planted as annuals and require six to eight hours of sun per day. You will also give them about one inch of water per week.

**How to Plant:**

1. Soil should be loosened and worked well after the last frost to ensure cucumbers won't experience cold weather. Add organic matter to the soil to enrich it. They will need 70 degrees Fahrenheit to 95 degrees Fahrenheit to thrive.
2. Your seed packet will give you the best instructions for spacing but most of the time rows will need about 3 to 4 feet in space to do well. You will also need a trellis that is about 6 feet in height.

3. Bury your seeds 1 inch deep with 6 inches in spacing. Immediately water on a gentle setting. Once your seedlings reach 4 inches tall, thin to one cucumber per 16 inches.
4. Manage pests as you keep the soil moist but not wet. Ensure weeds don't make their way into the area as well.
5. When the cucumbers are 6 to 8 inches in length they are ready to harvest. Use a knife to cut the cucumbers from the vines rather than twisting off. This will be fifty to seventy days after sowing.

### Summer Squash

Summer squash is coincidently a summer favorite. It's a light vegetable that goes with a lot of different dishes. They are grown as annuals and are going to need about six hours of sunlight per day. You want to enrich your soil with heaps of organic matter and compost. This vegetable does not tolerate any frost so sowing will be well after the last expected frost.

### How to Plant:

1. You will need about 2 feet in space between planting your seeds. You can also space your

rows with the exact same measurements. The seeds should be 1 inch deep into the ground.

2. When they begin to blossom, keep adding nutrient-rich organic matter to nourish the summer squash. Also, continue to water keeping the plant moist but not soggy.

3. This vegetable grows quickly and will be ready to harvest in about fifty to sixty days. They grow with a crookneck and can vary in size from 6 inches to 10 inches. Once the outer skin is glossy this is a tell-tale sign it is ready to harvest. You will need to use a sharp knife to cut from the vine.

### *Winter Squash*

We talk about summer squash a lot but it's worth bringing up winter squash. Technically speaking, it is an annual fruit rather than a vegetable. They will also need six hours of sunlight just like summer squash. However, they need slightly more water a week from 1 to 2 inches. They need warm weather so starting indoors is never a bad idea.

### How to Plant:

1. Winter squash should be sown indoors for three to four weeks before transplanting

outside for northern climates. This is so that they surpass the last expected frost. You should plant your seeds 1 inch deep. If you are indoors, use a grow light!

2. When moving them outside, ensure plenty of space because winter squash can be an acorn, butternut, pumpkin, or a number of other varieties. Regardless of your variant, water at the base rather than overhead.

3. Since squash is a heavy feeder, you need to keep reapplying heavy phosphorus and low nitrogen compost to nourish it. Keep an eye out for pests as, unfortunately, squash does attract a number of beetles.

4. When the stems begin to crack and dry this is a sign that your winter squash is ready to harvest. Leaving it on the vine for as long as possible right before the first frost is the best for harvesting. Use a sharp knife to cut the squash from the vine.

### Zucchini

Last but not least on our list is the veggie that gets confused with cucumbers all the time. Zucchini! These annuals will follow very similar planting behaviors as the others. Give them six to eight hours of sun for them to do well. They will also take 1 to 2 inches of water depending on how dry the soil is.

**How to Plant:**

1. You can direct sow into the soil when it has reached a temperature of 60 degrees Fahrenheit. Sow them 1 inch into the ground with 3 to 4 inches of space between seeds. Rows need 3 to 6 feet in space.
2. Give lots of water after planting the seeds and add a layer of compost to the top. This will help discourage weeds.
3. Following the other squash, you want to harvest when they are 6 to 8 inches in length as well. This will take about sixty days and you can use a sharp knife to harvest.

## ADDING VISIBLE DIVERSITY TO YOUR GARDEN

Vine plants are such a functional way to garden as they create a lot of free space by growing vertically. It's great for some vegetables that don't take up as much space as well. From an aesthetic appearance, they are also beautiful to look at and can bring a design element to your garden that creates zen and peace.

# 10

# HOW WILL HERBS HELP YOUR VEGETABLE GARDEN

If you are anything like me then you love the way herbs create an entirely different taste and feeling when eating a dish. For instance, imagine having your favorite spaghetti and meatball recipe. The marinara sauce has fresh basil coated on top and that's what makes it! Herbs are amazing for so many reasons. They taste great, they are easy to grow, and they can actually help keep pests out of our garden and away from other vegetables.

Another thing to consider when thinking about your garden is whether you should or should not grow herbs. Have you ever spent $5 or more on a spice or herb at the grocery store? Chances are you can pay a lot less and just make it yourself.

## HOW WILL HERBS HELP YOUR GARDEN?

We've spent some time talking about how to make our soil ready for the conditions our vegetables need. This includes all the organic matter and nutrients we have put into our compost system and methods. The last thing we want to do is to spray it with a bunch of pesticides. This can end up getting into our vegetables and cause us to ingest it! But pests and insects nonetheless are always going to be around. So how do we manage them?

Herbs are a great way to handle this. Herbs help deter pests in a natural and organic way. While we will later get into companion planting, it's important to know the benefits. Not only will your vegetables taste better but it is also better for the earth to not use chemicals.

## HOW WILL HERBS HELP YOU?

While herbs definitely play a healthier role in your garden, they also have a number of health benefits themselves from digesting them. And let's be honest, herbs can be the saving grace to a dinner dish that has taken a turn for the worst. When in doubt, bring the garlic out!

But let's check out some of these fun, healthy herb facts.

1. Did you know that **oregano** has 3 to 20 times higher antioxidant activity than any other herb. It also has 42 times more antioxidant levels of activity than an apple!
2. **Parsley** has so much vitamin K that a ¼ cup of it would give you more than two times your needed daily serving.
3. The antioxidants in **Rosemary** have been studied and found to be linked to anticancer properties.
4. **Coriander** has so many benefits it's hard to name them all. Digestive health and brain function are among the top two.

5. Besides a tasty herb, **garlic** also has many benefits including helping prevent Alzheimer's and dementia.

6. **Ginger** plays a big role in fighting off chronic diseases and has a positive effect on managing blood cholesterol levels.

There are so many herbs that offer a plethora of benefits that it's hard to have any justification for not adding them to our beautiful gardens!

## STARTING A HERB GARDEN AS AMAZING AS YOUR VEGETABLE GARDEN

Remember when we spoke about all the space between the rows in our vegetable garden? Well, we are finally going to find a use for them. So many gardeners think that perfect rows are the answer but actually, this is a waste of space! This is where your herbs belong and can help out your vegetables.

### *Basil*

Basil happens to be one of the most popular herbs in America. It's easy to start a basil seed indoors to get a jump start on the weather. It will grow best in six to eight hours of sunlight and count on about 1 inch of

water per week. Ironically enough, they make great companions with tomatoes.

**How to Plant:**

1. Consider starting your seed four to eight weeks inside before the last frost date. They won't tolerate cold weather so ensure, if you plan to direct sow, that it's safe from frost.
2. Sow your moist starter seed about ½ to 1 inch below the soil. Cover with ¼ dry starter seed mix. Water immediately with a spray bottle.
3. In your pots, provide some humidity by wrapping the top with plastic wrap. After you spot seedlings you can remove this.
4. When getting ready to transplant, amend your soil with tons of organic matter. Ensure there is at least 8 inches of depth for the root to grow and space plants 12 to 16 inches apart in a 6-inch hold. The root ball should be level with your soil.
5. Fill and water with 1 to 2 inches per week. You can start to punch true leaves to encourage

more growth and a fuller bush. After 3 to 4 weeks pinch your leaves and continue to harvest throughout the season.

## Chives

Think cream cheese. Chives are a strong herb that goes great with a lot of different things like chicken and fish. They also need six to eight hours of sun to thrive and will count on a thorough watering once to twice a week depending on the conditions. Chives are considered a fine herb along with parsley and tarragon.

**How to Plant:**

1. Consider starting your seed inside by planting ½ inch deep into a pot about four to six weeks before the last frost date.
2. If you want to direct sow, you need to space your seed 4 to 15 inches apart with a row space of 20 inches or more. This is because it grows into a bulb much like an onion.
3. The soil needs to be between pH 6 and 8 and rich in organic matter. Water deeply and continue to add things like grass clippings to retain moisture.

4. Chives are ready thirty days after transplanting or sixty if you direct sow. To harvest, snip the leaves from the base of the plant.

### *Dill*

Dill is a surprising herb in the sense that it is a perennial that reaches 2 to 4 feet in height. Its fresh or dried leaves are used for a number of things like dips, soups, salads, and much more. Interestingly enough, dill is one that thrives in not the best soil conditions. Like the others, dill needs six to eight hours of sunlight.

**How to Plant:**

1. Direct sow your seeds after the last frost has passed. Transplanting here won't work. Sow them ¾ to 1 inch deep and space them 12 to 15 inches apart.
2. However, you can grow them indoors and outdoors in containers if you do not want to direct sow. Regardless of indoors or outdoors, they need to be supported with a stake. Water 1 to 2 inches a week.

3. After about ninety days they will be ready to harvest. To do so you will need to clip them close to the stem early morning or late evening.

## Marjoram

This may be a herb you have not heard of before but, nonetheless, it's a goodie. It is a perennial herb that belongs to the mint family and has a balsam-pine-like taste often used in salads, soups, and Mediterranean dishes. It grows best in slightly acidic soil with good drainage.

**How to Plant:**

1. Using a seed starting kit, sow the seed eight to ten weeks indoors before the last frost date. Sow them about ¼ inch deep in soil that is about 70 degrees Fahrenheit.
2. You'll want to space these seeds about 12 inches apart. You can cover it with several inches of organic matter.
3. To encourage growth, trim buds back when they first appear. These plants will grow 12 to 24 inches tall.
4. Water every few days when the top of the soil is dry.

5. After four to six weeks it will be ready for harvest. To harvest, snip off the shoots and strip the leaves.

## Mint

Mint is a much more commonly known herb and can be used for a number of reasons. This fragrant perennial only needs three to four hours of sunlight a day to grow. Different from some other herbs, plan on hydrating it once or twice a day as mint needs plenty of water.

**How to Plant:**

1. Consider sowing indoors ¼ inch deep for eight to ten weeks before the last frost in spring. You can also sow directly outdoors in late spring.
2. Mint has lively roots so plant 12 inches to 24 inches apart in space. After ten to sixteen days you will notice sprouting.
3. For better growth, you want to prune back the plants in the early summer. The entire harvest cycle will take around ninety days and the plant will reach 1 to 2 feet in height.
4. Harvesting is super easy. All you have to do is pinch the leaf at the stem.

## *Oregano*

Oregano is another one of the most common herbs that we use in our beloved Italian dishes. Technically speaking, it is also a perennial and a member of the mint family. It will need six hours of full sun and about 1 inch of water per week. Though you need to let the soil dry out between waterings.

**How to Plant:**

1. When the weather is nice and warm (70 degrees Fahrenheit) you can direct sow seeds just on top of the soil surface level. There should be about 20 inches of space between the rows.
2. Oregano will do well in free-draining soil. Their care is relatively easy as you just need to water about one inch a week. Once you hit late spring you can cut back the plant ⅓ to make it even bushier.
3. It will be ready to harvest in mid-summer. You can snip the leaves at the stems then for the best flavor.

## *Parsley*

Parsley is actually one of those vegetables that can be a bit tricky to deal with. But once you get the hang of this biennial it's well worth it. There are also a few varieties of parsley but when it comes to cooking the dark green flat is the best to plant. Once it is established you'll find it very low maintenance. However, make sure they get six to eight hours of sun per day!

**How to Plant:**

1. When the soil is workable, direct sow four to six weeks before the average last frost date. You can check your zones to see when it's best for your area.
2. Before planting, consider soaking your seeds for twelve to twenty-four hours to help germination.
3. Plant 2 to 3 seeds together ¼ inch deep below the soil and cover lightly. Space your groupings 6-8 inches apart.
4. Gently water so you don't displace all the seeds.
5. Two seed leaves will be the first to appear. Then true leaves will follow after that. Between seventy and ninety days is when you will be able to snip the leaves off at the stems to harvest.

## *Rosemary*

Rosemary seeds are one of the slower herbs to germinate so it's recommended to start indoors three to six months before the growing season. Technically, it's a perennial but grown as an annual because of the winter season. They'll do well in a space that gives them six hours of sun.

**How to Plant:**

1. Small pots, egg cartons, or small containers all work when starting to sow indoors. Fill with a good organic mix and place three to four seeds on top. Lightly cover so they still have sunlight.
2. Use a spray bottle to lightly cover the seeds with water. Then cover the container with plastic wrap. You can uncover them when you see them start to emerge.
3. Once the rosemary reaches 3 inches high you can transplant it outdoors in a space that gets six to eight hours of sunlight per day.
4. Lightly water every one to two weeks. Rosemary has a usual 80 to 120-day range depending on whether you start indoors or outdoors. To harvest, cut at the stems right after the morning dew before the heat.

## *Coriander*

Did you know that cilantro and coriander come from the same plant? This makes growing either one incredibly efficient. It's a fast-growing annual herb that does better in cooler weather as opposed to other plants. Coriander needs about four to six hours of sunlight per day.

**How to Plant:**

1. To avoid bolting, plant in middle to late fall or early spring so you don't deal with the summer heat.
2. You can space the seeds about 1 to 2 inches apart with rows that have 12 inches of spacing.
3. Water about 1 inch per week to keep the seeds and soil nice and moist. At the same time thin your seedlings about 6 inches apart.
4. Once the plants appear above ground in full form, mulch around the base to prevent weeds from growing in.
5. Harvest once the seeds have dropped. You can either take the entire plant or cut smaller leaves off at the stem and large leaves individually.
6. Take the seeds by cutting off the heads and placing them in a paper bag to dry out.

## *Thyme*

Thyme is a multi-use herb that tastes great and is an awesome garnish. This perennial is relatively easy to grow but when working from seed can take a long time to germinate. Count on giving it five or more hours of direct sunlight. However, there won't be much watering which makes this herb slightly different.

**How to Plant:**

1. About twelve weeks before the last frost in spring, scatter your seeds across the top of the soil with the container you plan to grow your thyme seeds in.
2. Give it a gentle watering and cover with plastic wrap to keep the humidity in and help germination.
3. Place your container in a warm location as you wait for the seeds to germinate between 1 and 12 weeks.
4. Wait till your seedlings reach 4 inches high before you transplant them into the garden. Do not transplant until the last frost has passed.
5. Transplant into the ground and mulch around the base. Little water is needed. Once it reaches 6 inches in length you can harvest it by snipping off the leaves! It's that easy!

## LOW MAINTENANCE AND BIG BENEFITS

Herbs are such wonderful things to include in your vegetable garden because they require so little maintenance. And they fit in all the nooks and crannies of your garden so that no space goes unused! Besides a few of the herbs on the list, most of them are quick to germinate and you won't need to tend to them as often as you tend to some of the needier plants in your garden.

The best part about these herbs is that you can dry them all out and use them as spices and herbs for up to two years after harvesting. Or you can use them fresh and as you go! For me, the vegetables taste a whole lot better when the dishes are accompanied by that little kick of something!

# 11

# WHY YOUR VEGETABLES NEED FLOWERS

You are probably wondering if it is finally the time that we are going to start talking about companion planting and its benefits. If you don't know what companion planting is then don't worry because we still aren't quite there. This chapter is all about flowers and why they make such a massive impact on our vegetable gardens. The pollination effects that flowers have on our vegetables help create a healthy environment for our veggie friends.

And depending on what vegetables we are growing, they don't always offer the most attractive colors. But flowers can make a garden pop and look beautiful, overflowing our gardens with pink, yellow, orange, purple, red and so many more colors. I am someone who loves to be pleased aesthetically on top of having functional use for our gardens! There is nothing like looking out your window to see your hard work looking great.

## FLOWERS IN A VEGETABLE PATCH–MORE THAN JUST VISUALLY APPEALING

But flowers are so much more than just a visually appealing idea. Have you ever heard about the birds and the bees? OK, not that kind. The kind I am talking about is the animals and insects that do come to your garden to help pollinate it. This includes beautiful butterflies. And while pests like spiders and other insects don't sound great, we need them along with wasps and ladybugs to keep things in line. They act as pest control.

For example, our lovely tomatoes are self-pollinating so they don't need too much help. But other plants like garlic, onion, potatoes, and cabbages don't self-pollinate and need a boost. The three flying friends that could be a good help would be hummingbirds, bees, and butterflies. But these guys don't come around unless their favorite flowers happen to be there as well.

## FLOWERS TO CONSIDER GROWING IN YOUR VEGETABLE GARDEN

In this section, we are going to look at a handful of beneficial flowers that you can add to your garden for function and beauty. Not only will we learn how to plant them but it is important to understand why each flower is useful for your garden specifically.

### *Marigolds*

Marigolds are a brilliantly colored annual that bring fiery orange and yellows to your garden. Butterflies, bees, ladybugs, and a whole lot more beneficial insects will flock to these flowers as long as you give them a good sunny spot. Apparently, they also keep the deer away from eating nearby vegetables. To reap all of these benefits make sure the soil is well-draining and free of rocks and weeds.

**How to Plant:**

1. Marigolds germinate quickly and take about eight weeks to bloom. You want to plant your seeds after the danger of frost has passed in springtime.
2. Seeds can be sown with one inch of space in between them. Right after planting them, you can water them thoroughly. '
3. When the seeds sprout, you will want to thin them out according to your variety. French varieties will need to be 8 to 10 inches apart and African varieties need 10 to 12 inches in space.
4. Caring for marigolds is easy as long as you keep up the deadheading. This both looks better and encourages more blooming. Also water at the base of the plant and not overhead.

## *Borage*

Borage is more commonly known as bugloss and is a Mediterranean herb and flower that is grown as an annual. They are a beautiful bright blue with a star shaped-figure that is marvelous to look at. But they don't just look pretty, they are actually an edible herb that is often used as a garnish for fancy summer drinks and food. Borage will need full sun but is relatively easy to plant and maintain. Borage should be planted mid-spring.

**How to Plant:**

1. Borage has large black seeds that can be directly sown right into the soil. Since they form deep roots they don't do well as transplanted flowers. It requires well-draining soil that is low in fertility.
2. Sow about two inches deep into the soil. After quick germination, thin your seedlings to 12 inches in space. Keep the soil moist with water every few days.
3. Cut off the deadheads to keep encouraging new blooms. Leave it in your garden or harvest it by snipping at the stem.

### *Nasturtiums*

Whenever a seed is directly sown into the ground it is a good sign that they are easy to care for and grow. Nasturtiums are just that. These beautiful flowers come in red, yellow, or orange and are, interestingly enough, edible as well. They are commonly known as the trap crop for luring in squash bugs and more insects that are a little too nosy in your vegetable garden. Ultimately, they are most loved for their common attractor of great pollinators. But in order for that to work, they require at least eight hours of full sun to do well.

**How to Plant:**

1. Sow seeds two weeks before the last frost with 8 to 12 inches of space in between and about 1 ½ inches deep into your soil. Cover with soil to germinate.
2. Thin your seedlings when they have their first set of true leaves. Water the soil to about 6 inches in depth.
3. That's it! Easy. If you want to harvest, wait till the flowers have fully sprouted. The petals are edible.

*Calendula*

Calendula is known as pot marigold and you will notice the red, orange, and yellow flowers have a lot of similar qualities. What makes them beautiful is their double ring petals. Interestingly enough, they are not directly related to marigolds. In order to take advantage of all the pollinators and visitors they get, you will need to put them in direct sun or part shade if the summers get very hot. In the hottest climates, they will not thrive.

**How To Plant:**

1. Calendula will do best when they are put in rich soil with organic matter. However, too much nitrogen will cause foliage rather than growth and budding.
2. Plant your seed with around 5 inches of space between them so they can grow without competing with each other. They should be placed about ½ inch below the surface of the soil.
3. Water regularly while also adding a layer of organic compost to the space every so often to keep the soil rich. All that's left is to deadhead when needed.

## Sunflowers

Sunflowers are a fan favorite and are really the symbol of joy and sunshine. These big bright flowers will last you an entire summer and have so many benefits when you add them to your vegetable garden. They attract some great birds because of their seeds and oil. And when they are done bringing in the birds and bees, they also make great flowers to cut and bring into your kitchen.

**How to Plant:**

1. It's no shocker that they need a lot of sun every day. They also need well-draining soil and you will have to prepare a bed for them that is 2 feet deep and 3 feet wide.
2. Since they are also heavy feeders they are going to need a lot of organic matter to keep growing.
3. Sow seeds directly into the ground after the danger of frost has passed. They need to be planted 1 ½ inches deep with about 6 inches of space in between the flowers. Rows will need about 30 inches.
4. Water around the plant roots 3 to 4 inches away from the base of the plant. As the plant becomes established, water both infrequently but deeply when you do.

*Lavender*

Lavender is one of the scents we love to fill our homes and our laundry detergents. Unlike some of the other flowers we have listed, lavender is actually a perennial plant. They have up-right flower spikes showing beautiful purples, greens, and greys. While native to Europe, it is commonly planted in the spring in North America. While it certainly can help your garden, you can also take advantage of the flower to get a better night's sleep, add to your coffee, reduce blood pressure, and a number of other amazing benefits.

**How to Plant:**

1. Lavender works with almost any plant if they get full sun and soil that is alkaline. However, they tolerate many conditions well.
2. Direct sow your seeds ½ inch to 1 inch apart and lightly on top of the soil. You don't need to bury them. At first, water the seeds thoroughly but as they begin to sprout into seedlings back off the water.
3. Prune every spring even if you harvest them in the summer.

*Sweet Peas*

Sweet Peas are another fan favorite and that's due to their beautiful colors and fragrant smells which fill up the gardens. Not only are they great plants for cutting and bringing indoors but because their smell is so strong and nice, they attract a lot of visitors as well. Like most other flowers, they really need about six hours of sun to look and feel great.

**How to Plant:**

1. Unless you live in incredibly hot conditions, you can sow seeds in the springtime.
2. Soak your seeds for twenty-four hours before planting, as this helps the germination process.
3. Find pots with a lot of space for their deep roots. You can sow two seeds per pot. Push them about a ½ inch deep into the soil. Cover them with plastic wrap for humidity.
4. Once they reach about 4 to 6 inches, you can pinch the central growing tip to encourage branching.
5. Apply nutrient-rich organic compost to the plant beds before transplanting. You will also need to place a trellis or posts for the vines to climb upward.
6. You can plant the seedlings on either side of the trellis with eight inches of space. Continue to give consistent moisture as they bloom.

## *Lupins*

Lupins can easily be mistaken for lavender as they look very similar. They also grow vertically and can be mistaken for sweet peas as well. But lupins bring their own benefits to the table. They can be purple, blue, pink, yellow, or white, which brings a variety of colors to your garden. They are short-lived perennials but require some of the least care out of all the flowers.

**How to Plant:**

1. Loosen your soil 12 to 20 inches deep in a sunny spot to plant your lupins in early spring.
2. Soak your seeds for twenty-four hours to speed up the germination process.
3. Plant seeds ⅛ deep in the soil and lightly cover. Give them 1 inch of water every week. Then you don't need to do much besides pinching off deadheads. That's really it.

*Comfrey*

Comfrey is actually a shrub and one that you have likely come across but wouldn't recognize immediately by name. Interestingly enough, this shrub can grow up to 5 feet tall and has purple, blue, and white flowers sprouting throughout the shrub. The roots and leaves of comfrey are often used in traditional medicine for different types of pain. Along with the fact that they are great attracting pollinators and the right pest-controlling predatory insects, comfrey has a lot of good use.

**How to Plant:**

1. Give comfreys lots of space as you don't want to crowd out other plants in your garden.
2. Direct sow outdoors about three weeks before the average last frost date. Push the seeds about ½ inch deep into the soil.
3. Water consistently for three weeks keeping the soil moist. You do not need to feed comfreys. This is all the maintenance you need to do.

*Cosmos*

Last but certainly not least on the list are cosmos. And they are not the New York drink many are wishing for after 5 PM. The oil from cosmos attracts a lot of guests but it's also been used to treat Malaria in Mexico and other countries. They look very much like a daisy and are a cute and colorful option to add to the garden. They will do best in full sun unless it's brutally hot conditions. These are one of the easiest plants to sow.

**How to Plant:**

1. Plant after the last frost has passed and space seeds 10 to 12 inches apart.

2. They don't need to be overwatered as they prefer drier soil. But until well-established, keep them slightly moist.
3. When the first bloom hits, cut them back to encourage more branching and blooming. Simple as that.

## EASY PEASY!

Flowers are such an easy addition to your garden because most of them can be planted and watered with little more maintenance required. They bring so many benefits such as looking good and pollinating your vegetables to help them grow and be healthy. And some of the above flowers even have links to traditional medicine and can be used in other areas for health and beauty benefits. Planting flowers in the garden is the perfect way to companion plants, which we are finally getting closer to talking about.

# 12

# BRINGING IT ALL TOGETHER WITH COMPANION PLANTING

We have gone through several chapters on what vegetables to plant and where. With different needs for each one, it is easy to get overwhelmed. We don't need to stress too much as we can look at companion plants and simply remember that X goes great next to Y. This is where we will go back to the sun design of our garden. That's the first thought. We also want to consider what goes together in terms of who will go in raised beds, grow bags, or be directly sown into the ground. When we do this right, we can have better-tasting and fresher crops.

## WHAT IS COMPANION PLANTING?

First, let's actually talk about what companion planting is. Companion planting is a technique and gardening strategy that sets your garden up for the most success because some plants will encourage others to grow while others don't make the best neighbors. The goal is that both plants will mutually benefit from being planted near or next to each other based on what they need and how they grow. If only one benefit, that still technically counts.

There are a lot of reasons for companion planting but let's go over a few of the most common ones.

1. Companion planting is usually your best defense against pests. Some plants will deter pests from the plants around them that are usual visitors.
2. It can have a positive effect on the soil, such as a nitrogen-fixing plant can help out non-nitrogen-fixing plants. In other words, it can help absorb the nitrogen when there is too much.
3. We never made this an option under trellis', but a tall plant can act as a trellis for smaller plants that need support. Or they can both offer each other support.

4. Taller plants can also provide some shade for other plants that need protection from strong sun and heat.

5. Weed control is one of the most popular ones, as those better-tasting help keep weeds out of the area.

Ultimately, when these things are in place then we can benefit as the gardener because our amount of work reduces. However, many people make the mistake of throwing anything together. This is especially true when we make the mistake of throwing vegetables from the same family or that sound like they may go together. The best example is potatoes and tomatoes. Because they require the same nutrients, the two of them will drain all of the nutrients from the soil, leaving an abundance of others. This means that the soil ultimately will become unhealthy, and so will the vegetables. You need vegetables that can make trade-offs. But as we talked about in our benefits, if you plant a very tall plant, this may provide safety for vine plants. Let's talk more specifically about combinations that work.

## WHICH VEGETABLES PAIR WELL TOGETHER?

Even though companion planting is a widely accepted practice, there is still a lot of hearsay and folklore about which combinations make sense and which don't. Here is a list of common vegetables and what benefits they get with their companion plants. You will see that the list is not limited to vegetables but flowers also make great companion planting.

### Asparagus

Asparagus does particularly well with a number of companions. In terms of vegetables, tomatoes are one of them. But if you want to add some flowers around them, Calendulas and Petunias are two of the best ones to choose from. The three of these companions deter asparagus beetles.

### Beans

Beans have a long list of friends, which is great for planting. You can use beets, sunflowers, corn, lovage, squash, strawberries, rosemary, and nasturtium. Nasturtiums help deter aphids from eating the beans. Lovage and rosemary have insect-repellent qualities. Sunflowers provide perfect shade. Corn will benefit from the bean's nitrogen-fixing ability.

## Beets

Brassicas, bush beans, garlic, lettuce, and the onion family are all companion plants for beets. Beets are also companions for chicory and endive. Onions will protect against borers and cutworms. Beets also add a significant amount of magnesium and nutrients to the soil.

## Broccoli

Broccoli has companions in the brassica family, like cabbage, brussel sprouts, cauliflower, etc. An herb that does particularly well is oregano because of its insecticidal properties. However, brassicas do well together, so you can net them. *Extra tip: add some lime to the soil.*

## Cabbage

You can use garlic, nasturtium, and a safe companion plant with cabbage. We know nasturtium deters beetles and aphids but also repels insects because of its strong odor. Sage particularly deters cabbage moths.

## Carrots

This is a long list. Chives, leeks, onions, peas, radishes, rosemary, and sage. Chives make the growth and flavor of carrots better while also deterring mites, aphids, and flies. Rosemary and sage work together to repel carrot flies. Leeks also have been said to repel many flying pests such as carrot rust fly.

## Corn

Pole beans, dill, cucumbers, melon, peas, squash, and sunflower, are all great companions for corn. Dill works to protect against aphids and mites. Beans work to bring more nitrogen. We know that sunflowers provide shade and structure. And to top it off, spinach actually grows great with corn.

## Cucumber

Beans, borage, dill, lettuce, nasturtiums, oregano, radish, sunflowers, and tansy are all on the long list of cucumbers. We know that nasturtium helps deter pests along with oregano. But tansy and radish help, particularly with cucumber beetles. Tansy and borage help with flavor as well.

## Lettuce

Chives, oregano, peas, poached egg plants, radishes, onions, scallions, and zinnia all make the cut for lettuce. Basil, as we know, provides great flavor to those around it. Poached egg plants such as a wildflower bring beneficial insects that eat aphids.

## Onions

Beets, cabbage, carrot, chard, lettuce, strawberry, and tomatoes are companions for onions. Onions, in particular, cut against borers and cutworms while also benefiting from marigolds, interestingly enough.

## Peas

Peas have one of the longest lists of companion plants. Alyssum, carrot, chives, corn, grapes, lettuce, mint, radish, spinach, and turnip. Chives will deter aphids. Mint brings the flavor. Alyssum brings pollinators and encourages green lacewings that eat aphids.

*Tip: Don't plant near onions and garlic.*

## Peppers

Basil, marjoram, onion, and oregano are companions of peppers. Basil, marjoram, and oregano have a protective insecticidal property.

## Potatoes

Basil, beans, calendula, horseradish, oregano, peas, tansy, catmint, cilantro, and garlic are all a part of the companions for potatoes. Beans help improve the size of potato tubers. Cilantro protects against mites, spiders, aphids, and more. Horseradish, calendula, and tansy planted at the corners of the patches ward of Colorado potato beetles.

## Radish

Chervil, peas, lettuce, and nasturtium are great for radishes. Chervil helps improve the growth and flavor of radishes, while peas give off nitrogen to the soil and plant. Radishes themselves are a trap crop.

## Squash/Pumpkins

Pole beans, buckwheat, calendula, corn, marigold, oregano, and nasturtium are great for squash and pumpkins. Buckwheat does a great job of bringing pest predators. Squash is also usually planted with corn and beans, which are commonly referred to as the three sisters.

## Tomatoes

Asparagus, borage, basil, calendula, dill, garlic, nasturtium, onion, parsley, and thyme. Thyme is a new one on our list that reduces egg-laying armyworms. The name alone sounds like an apocalypse. Basil also repels a long list of insects not wanted in your garden.

**Zucchini**

Buckwheat, zinnia, oregano, and nasturtium are for zucchini. We are now familiar with all of their benefits, but they make great companions for many vegetables.

## HOW TO CHOOSE THE BEST HERBS TO GROW WITH YOUR VEGETABLES

We've mentioned some herbs that are worth adding to your garden but let's look at some of them a little more closely.

**Basil**

Companions - Tomatoes, peppers, oregano, and asparagus.
Basil helps improve flavor while repelling insects.

**Chives**

Companions - Carrots, dill, tomatoes, and most herbs.
Repels aphids.

## Coriander

Companions - Legumes, dill, potatoes, and most herbs
Repels insects while also bringing nutrition to your soil.

## Sage

Companions - Rosemary.
Repels some beetles.

## Dill

Companions - Onion, corn, lettuce, cucumbers, and fennel.
Repels aphids, spiders, and other mites.

## Rosemary

Companions - Beans, pepper, broccoli, cabbage, and sage.
Rosemary helps deter a variety of pests.

## Parsley

Companions - Peas, onions, roses, and carrots.
Helps attract butterflies, hoverflies, and wasps.

**Thyme**

Companions - Eggplants. strawberries, cabbage, and potatoes.
Thyme attracts bees and other predatory insects.

## A BEAUTIFUL NOTE ON FLOWERS

One of the most important takeaways you can get from this chapter and the last is that flowers really have an amazing impact on your garden. A few are already mentioned in these companion lists above. However, we can't forget about some of the other popular friends. Here are some of the most popular. You'll recognize a few.

- Borage
- Calendula
- Cosmos
- Lavender
- Marigolds
- Nasturtiums

With these flowers and the herbs listed alongside the vegetables, we can get a pretty good look at the most popular companion combinations. However, it's nearly impossible to list them all because there are literally thousands of combinations that work. A quick Google search can tell you about the specific veggie or plant you are working with. From here, you can get inspired to create fun combinations of your own, but it is important to never forget to check the hardiness zones so you know when you can plant them. It's sort of like a checklist that becomes more familiar as you gain experience.

13

# GET THE MOST OUT OF YOUR GARDEN CROPS FOR YEAR-ROUND SELF-SUSTAINABILITY

There is nothing quite as exciting as seeing your seedlings come to fruition. However, the excitement can't end there, as sustaining your garden and maintaining it is the secret for success year after year. Being green is an accomplishment in itself, and when you're sustainable, you can take advantage of high yields without wasting much. This chapter is dedicated to the tricks and tips that will keep your garden ready to go year after year.

## WHAT IS TRANSPLANT SHOCK?

Naturally, if you were to move homes, there is both excitement and the stress of packing everything up and settling it into a new space. Plants get just as stressed when they have to move from indoor to outdoor spaces or even from one section of the garden to another. This is commonly known as transplant shock.

**Transplant Shock:** There are three factors to consider. The first is that the plant has undergone physical abuse. The second is a reduction in size. And lastly, is when it ends up in a new environment.

The third reason is the most common for us as we encourage colder climates to grow indoors and transplant later outdoors. Transplant shock is not hard to spot. Often the leaves will start to willow, the branches appear to be dying, and the fruit, vegetables, or leaves may abruptly fall. In the worst case, the plant dies altogether. This happens when we aren't careful about transplanting our seedlings and moving our plants. It also occurs when there is too much wind, sun, abrasive weather, etc.

Here is how to minimize your transplant damage:

1. Knowing when to transplant is half the battle. We spoke about ensuring you transplant after the frost. This is one of the more common culprits for plants that die. Also, transplanting when the seedlings are not ready can be harmful.

2. Do not disturb your roots. That's why container planting can be easier than grow bags. You want to let the roots stay firmly planted in the soil. Disrupting them can cause a lot of different issues and transplanting shock. If you have to disturb your roots, you want to take as many as possible to keep the plant healthy.

3. Next, you need to consider your environment. Going indoors to outdoors is a harsh change which is why you need to be mindful of the wind and sun. Giving them water to get settled is also important in the direction of each plant.

4. Lastly, hardening off your seedlings is a great way to minimize the damage. Hardening off just means that you will slowly introduce your seedlings to the outdoor climate to progressively get them ready for transplanting.

## TAKING CARE OF YOUR TOOLS

Taking care of your tools is a big part of learning how to become a seasoned gardener. Many beginners make the common mistake of using the same tools on diseased plants with healthy ones. This spreads disease and can lead to killing your healthy ones. Here, it is important to review the basic tips and tricks for keeping your tools as healthy as your plants.

The main thing to remember is that your stools need to be sterilized regularly. It's hard to tell sometimes when you come into contact with a disease! An easy way to combat this is to bring a shallow bucket of disinfectant and water to dip your tools into. It's important to make sure they aren't chemical-loaded because this can kill your plants. You can find special sanitizers sold in home improvement and garden stores.

Here are a few things you can use when going through a thorough cleaning:

**Bleach**

Mix one part bleach to nine parts water to create a cleaning solution for your gardening tools. Soak your tools for thirty minutes.

**Isopropyl Alcohol**

With this kind of treatment, you don't need to soak your tools. You can simply spray it on and wipe it down and your tools are ready to go.

**Household Cleaners**

Listerine, Lysol, and other common cleaners are sometimes used for gardening tools. Dilute them to ensure
you don't harm your plants after cleaning.

## WILL DRY FARMING WORK FOR ME?

This is a common question that frequently gets asked.
Dry farming really isn't about not watering your plants.
It's actually about taking advantage of moist soil that
already contains enough water. But dry farming
requires a level of timing that can be tricky. Normally,
this happens during wetter months. If you want to take
this approach, you will need to make sure the last frost
has passed, and you can count on some rain coming in
in the next three days. The rain helps the germination
process.

This is very common for spring weather. As summer
starts to approach, their roots will start to develop
around 80 to 90 degrees in temperature. The result is
that your roots will grow down instead of upwards to
get the water and firmly plant themselves. This works
for areas that are not dry and see a lot of spring
showers.

## SUCCESSION PLANTING FOR A LONGER HARVESTING SEASON

Someone who is new to gardening may be apt to plant all seeds at once. Unless you have a super large family, planting thirty seeds at once will result in too much food and waste. However, if you use something called succession planting, you can space out the harvesting and enjoy it in moderate amounts. This means planting a new batch every one to two weeks during the right season. This can also be called staggered planting.

Not all plants do well with succession planting. So consider these top vegetables that do!

- Kale
- Cauliflower
- Cabbage
- Carrots
- Onion
- Garlic
- Beets
- Potatoes

## CROP ROTATION AND ITS ADVANTAGES

Crop rotation means moving your crops around to different areas of your garden. The reason behind this is to keep your soil as fresh as possible so that plants don't eat up all the nutrients. It allows plants to come in and nourish with new nutrients and so on. Consider a simple three-year rotation to get the job done.

In your first year, you can grow nightshades in mulched soil. This prepares the soil for year two. In year two, you will transition the soil to a transitional bed where you can grow brassicas. Your brassicas will help get rid of weeds in the soil and prepare the area for year three. In the third year, you can have weed-free soil, which helps crops that are particularly sensitive to weeds.

## TO TILL OR NOT TO TILL

As with anything, there are pluses and minuses when it comes to tilling. While tilling has short-term effects to get the vegetable gardens ready quicker, leaving it alone can have better long-term results for garden health. So, when should you do it, and when do you leave it alone?

- When you till, you should be doing it for a specific purpose, such as incorporating organic matter into the soil.
- If you have done a good job mulching for the past few years, then don't worry about tilling. When the soil is in good condition, leave it alone.

This brings us to the topic of mulching.

## WHY YOU SHOULD BE MULCHING

Nobody likes it when the sun and heat turn your beautiful soil into a dust pit. Mulching can prevent that from happening because it keeps your soil moist and full of nutrients. Some people believe that mulching is simply adding organic matter, but that's not true. There are many types of mulches, such as straw, leaves, cardboard, woodchips, and compost. All of them can help suppress weed growth, so your vegetables don't fight for space.

## WHAT IS SEED STRATIFICATION?

Seed stratification is a way to begin germination and end dormancy. Essentially, we are pre-treating our seeds to set them up for success. We can do this in two ways: the moist version and the dry version.

Dry stratification is when you expose your seed to temperatures below 32 degrees Fahrenheit. This lasts for about a month or a little longer. There are a certain number of seeds that specifically need the dry method. All you need to do is put them in ziplock bags in the refrigerator.

Moist stratification is when you expose the seeds to cold and damp conditions over the winter months. You'll need to immerse it with moist sawdust, builder's sand, or other similar materials to get the effect. However, if you direct plant in the fall, you get the same effects, so it is really not necessary to do.

## INSPIRATION FOR STORING YOUR VEGETABLES

The best part of growing your food is that you will have plenty of leftovers. But they don't last long if you don't store them the right way. Just remember that certain veggies and fruit store better than others.

Like:

- Root veggies
- Apples and pears
- Squash family
- Onion, garlic, and shallots (dried then stored in dry container)
- Legumes (if frozen or dried and stored in an airtight container, are good for over a year)
- Berries (freeze well)

One that doesn't do well is leafy greens. These need to be consumed immediately within three to four days.

# Please Leave a Review!

Dear Valued Readers,
We hope you have enjoyed and benefited from the content we bring to you. As authors, we pour our hearts and souls into creating engaging and thought-provoking pieces that resonate with you. Today, we would like to kindly ask for a moment of your time to consider leaving a review about our work. Your reviews hold immense significance for us as authors. They provide valuable insight into what aspects of our writing resonate with you and what areas we can improve upon. Therefore, by leaving a review, you contribute to our growth and success. We sincerely appreciate your support and the time you invest in sharing your thoughts. Thank you for your time.
Warmest regards,
Noor Fatima

# TIE IT ALL TOGETHER WITH
# A BOW

In this book, you will learn how to garden and avoid the most common beginner mistakes. It seems like a lot of information (which it is) but as you practice it, you will see that the information flows together naturally when you are going through the steps. For me, gardening growing up was a connection between my aunts and uncles, and dad. I fostered an early love for this practice. When I learned, it was not only good for me but good for the earth and the connection only grew stronger. I found techniques that really worked and learned a lot along the way. That's why it was so important for me to share this with you!

Regardless of how well you follow this book, there are going to be mistakes made. It's patience and love for the garden that will help you reset onto the right path. This is why having a calendar or an app can be particularly useful for reminders and staying organized as much as possible. Each plant has a unique set of timelines and practices. Some work well together while others will keep and kill each other. Having something to refer back to like a summary of those plants can be the reason things go right.

It's important, even if you have notes, to start small. Especially if this is your first plant ever, working with one or two plants and adding more as soon as you master the basic steps is the right way to start. Even just getting the right type of soil can be tricky at first. This sets you up to become familiar with the terminology and basics right off the bat.

Without designing your garden, it's also easy to misplant the veggies or plants. More often than not, depending on your climate, you need to start your seedlings indoors until they're ready to be hardened off by the climate. Starting at the very beginning is how you will either succeed or get off track. That's why it can even have many trials a little before you have your first success.

The best thing you can do is just start with a seed and practice with that one plant. It's that simple! That's how you learn to become a gardener.

I hope that this book brings you as much joy as it did for me to write it. After many many years of trial and error, I believe I have one of the most straightforward and easy-to-apply practices out there. But it's not just about reaping benefits, being environmentally sound, or picking up a hobby. It's about learning to connect with yourself and our beautiful earth.

I hope you find this, and whether you loved it or found something difficult to understand, please leave a review and let me know what you think. That way we can improve the formula of success together!

Thank you,

Noor Fatima

# Just for You

## A free Gift for our Readers

The Green Thumb's Guide: Naturally
Controlling Garden Pests

# REFERENCE SHEET

## INTRODUCTION

Lacerda, C. (2020, July 26). *Create Your Life with the 1 Percent Rule.* Medium. https://medium.com/@ceciliaalacerda/create-your-life-with-the-1-percent-rule-9b22a83a921d

*How to Start a Vegetable Garden | Small Space, Tight Budget Gardening.* (2020, April 8). https://extramile.thehartford.com/home/landscaping-and-gardening/vegetable-garden/

*The Only Tools You Need to Start a Garden.* (n.d.). EatingWell. https://www.eatingwell.com/article/17068/the-only-tools-you-need-to-start-a-garden/

*Common Gardening Terms.* (n.d.). Botanical Interests. https://www.botanicalinterests.com/product/Garden-Glossary

January 17, M. O., & 2020. (n.d.). *Take a Tour of Martha's Most Beautiful Gardens and Learn How She Created Each of Them.* Martha Stewart. Retrieved December 5, 2022, from https://www.marthastewart.com/7982450/common-gardening-terms-beginners

*Find out your soil type.* (n.d.). BBC Gardeners' World Magazine. https://www.gardenersworld.com/plants/find-out-your-soil-type/

https://www.facebook.com/thespruceofficial. (2018). *Test the Acidity of Your Soil Without a Pricey Kit.* The Spruce. https://www.thespruce.com/how-to-test-soil-acidity-alkalinity-without-a-test-kit-1388584

*Making Soil More Acidic Organically | Kellogg Garden OrganicsTM.* (n.d.). Kellogggarden.com. https://kellogggarden.com/blog/soil/how-to-make-soil-more-acidic-organically/

US EPA. (2018, October 16). *Composting at home.* US EPA. https://www.epa.gov/recycle/composting-home

EarthEasy. (2019). *Composting.* Eartheasy Guides & Articles. https://learn.eartheasy.com/guides/composting/

Jowaheer, R. (2019, September 2). *10 steps for making your own compost heap at home.* Country Living. https://www.countryliving.com/uk/homes-interiors/gardens/a23333516/how-to-make-compost-heap-home/

DebWFF. (2019, March 1). *What Is a Hardiness Zone, and Why Is It Important?* White Flower Farm's Blog. https://www.whiteflowerfarm.com/blog/2019/03/01/what-is-a-hardiness-zone-and-why-is-it-important/

https://www.facebook.com/thespruceofficial. (2019). *Find Your USDA Zone With These State Maps.* The Spruce. https://www.thespruce.com/find-your-usda-zone-3269819

https://www.facebook.com/thespruceofficial. (2019). *Find Your USDA Zone With These State Maps.* The Spruce. https://www.thespruce.com/find-your-usda-zone-3269819

*Mini Greenhouse Gardening - How To Use A Mini Greenhouse.* (n.d.). Gardening Know How. Retrieved December 5, 2022, from https://www.gardeningknowhow.com/special/greenhouses/mini-greenhouse-information.htm

*Turnip Seed to Harvest : Urban Farmer Seeds.* (n.d.). Www.ufseeds.com. Retrieved December 5, 2022, from https://www.ufseeds.com/turnip-seed-to-harvest.html

Old Farmer's Almanac. (2019, July 4). *Radishes.* Old Farmer's Almanac. https://www.almanac.com/plant/radishes

GardeningChannel. (2015, February 26). *How to Grow Kale: Including Three Favorite Ways to Prepare Kale.* Gardening Channel. https://www.gardeningchannel.com/how-to-grow-kale-including-three-favorite-ways-to-prepare-kale/

Albert, S. (2009). *How to Grow Cabbage In Easy Steps.* Harvest to Table. https://harvesttotable.com/how_to_grow_cabbage/

*Growing, Harvesting & Enjoying Mustard Greens.* (2017, September 14). Hobby Farms. https://www.hobbyfarms.com/mustard-greens-growing-gardening/

gardeningchannel. (2010, March 9). *How to Grow Cauliflower.* Gardening Channel. https://www.gardeningchannel.com/how-to-grow-cauliflower/

Heber, G. (2019, February). *Gardener's Path*. Gardener's Path. https://gardenerspath.com/plants/vegetables/brussels-sprouts/

*How To Grow Watercress | Thompson & Morgan*. (n.d.). Www.thompson-Morgan.com. Retrieved December 5, 2022, from https://www.thompson-morgan.com/how-to-grow-watercress

*StackPath*. (n.d.). Www.gardeningknowhow.com. https://www.gardeningknowhow.com/edible/vegetables/bok-choy/bok-choy-harvesting.htm

*Leafy Greens: Health Benefits*. (n.d.). Almanac.com. Retrieved December 5, 2022, from https://www.almanac.com/go-leafy-greens

Albert, S. (2022, June 8). *How to Plant, Grow, and Harvest Cardoon*. Harvest to Table. https://harvesttotable.com/how_to_grow_cardoon/

*Chichory Seed to Harvest - Urban Farmer Seeds*. (n.d.). Www.ufseeds.com. https://www.ufseeds.com/chicory-seed-to-harvest.html

*Growing Globe Artichokes - How to Grow Globe Artichokes*. (n.d.). Allotment & Gardens. Retrieved December 5, 2022, from https://www.allotment-garden.org/vegetable/globe-artichokes-growing/

Old Farmer's Almanac. (2019, April 4). *Lettuce*. Old Farmer's Almanac. https://www.almanac.com/plant/lettuce

*How to grow Swiss chard*. (n.d.). BBC Gardeners World Magazine. Retrieved December 5, 2022, from https://www.gardenersworld.com/how-to/grow-plants/how-to-grow-swiss-chard-2/

*Beets - How do you know when beets are ready to harvest?* (n.d.). Texas A&M AgriLife Extension Service. https://agrilifeextension.tamu.edu/library/gardening/beets/

Old Farmer's Almanac. (2019, July 5). *Corn*. Old Farmer's Almanac. https://www.almanac.com/plant/corn

*How to Grow Asparagus - Planting Asparagus | Gardener's Supply*. (n.d.). Gardeners Supply. https://www.gardeners.com/how-to/growing-asparagus/7343.html

*Health Benefits of Legumes*. (n.d.). WebMD. https://www.webmd.com/food-recipes/health-benefits-legumes

*How to Grow Chickpeas*. (n.d.). WikiHow. https://www.wikihow.com/Grow-Chickpeas

*Growing Peas From Sowing to Harvest*. (n.d.). GrowVeg. Retrieved December 5, 2022, from https://www.growveg.com/guides/grow ing-peas-from-sowing-to-harvest/

Griffiths, M. (2021, October 1). *How to grow kidney beans – a healthy inclusion to the home garden*. Homesandgardens.com. https://www. homesandgardens.com/advice/how-to-grow-kidney-beans

Grant, A. (2018, April 4). *How to Grow Pinto Beans: Care And Harvesting Of Pintos*. Gardening Know How. https://www.gardening knowhow.com/edible/vegetables/beans/how-to-grow-pinto-beans.htm

*Growing Lentils: Protein-Packed Legumes*. (2020, May 26). Epic Gardening. https://www.epicgardening.com/growing-lentils/

*Growing Green Beans - How to Grow Pole Beans, Bush Beans*. (n.d.). Www.gardeners.com. https://www.gardeners.com/how-to/beans/ 7156.html

*How to Grow Lima Beans | The Dirt Blog | Stauffers of Kissel Hill*. (2018, March 29). Stauffers. https://www.skh.com/thedirt/how-to-grow-lima-beans/

*How to Grow Peanuts*. (n.d.). Harvest to Table. https://harvesttotable. com/how_to_grow_peanuts/

chuck.mcmullan. (2020, November 28). *Potato Growing and Harvest Information*. VeggieHarvest.com. https://veggieharvest.com/vegeta bles/potato-growing-and-harvest-information/

*Growing Potatoes in Grow Bags from Planting to Harvest*. (n.d.). Squire's Garden Centres. Retrieved December 5, 2022, from https://www. squiresgardencentres.co.uk/garden_advice/growing-potatoes-in-grow-bags-from-planting-to-harvest/#

*Tomatoes: Planting, Growing and Harvesting*. (2012, December 8). Planet Natural. https://www.planetnatural.com/growing-tomato-plants/

*Growing Cherry Tomatoes – Planting And Picking Cherry Tomatoes*. (n.d.). Gardening Know How. https://www.gardeningknowhow.com/ edible/vegetables/tomato/growing-cherry-tomatoes.htm

Almanac, O. F. (n.d.). *Eggplants*. Old Farmer's Almanac. https://www. almanac.com/plant/eggplants

*How to grow chillies*. (n.d.). BBC Gardeners World Magazine. https://

www.gardenersworld.com/how-to/grow-plants/how-to-grow-peppers-and-chillies/

Heber, G. (2019, January 30). *How to Grow and Harvest Tomatillos | Gardener's Path*. Gardener's Path. https://gardenerspath.com/plants/vegetables/tomatillos/

Denenberg, Z. (n.d.). *Everything You Need to Know about Root Vegetables*. Southern Living. https://www.southernliving.com/food/side-dishes/vegetables/what-are-root-vegetables

*How to Grow Carrots*. (2009, February 16). Harvest to Table. https://harvesttotable.com/how_to_grow_carrots/

*Ginger - How long does it take to grow and harvest ginger?* (n.d.). Texas A&M AgriLife Extension Service. https://agrilifeextension.tamu.edu/library/gardening/ginger/

*How to Grow Onions*. (2009, January 24). Harvest to Table. https://harvesttotable.com/how_to_grow_onion/

*How to Plant, Grow and Harvest Garlic*. (n.d.). GardenTech.com. https://www.gardentech.com/blog/gardening-and-healthy-living/how-to-grow-your-own-garlic

*How to grow parsnips | Thompson & Morgan*. (n.d.). Www.thompson-Morgan.com. Retrieved December 5, 2022, from https://www.thompson-morgan.com/how-to-grow-parsnips

*Growing and Caring for Sweet Potatoes*. (n.d.). The Spruce. https://www.thespruce.com/how-to-grow-sweet-potatoes-in-the-home-garden-1403479

*Fennel : From Seeds To Harvest - Urban Farmer Seeds*. (n.d.). Www.ufseeds.com. Retrieved December 5, 2022, from https://www.ufseeds.com/fennel-seed-to-harvest.html

*Characteristics of Vines*. (n.d.). Sciencing. https://sciencing.com/characteristics-of-vines-13426425.html

*10 DIY Garden Trellises That Cost Less Than $20*. (n.d.). The Spruce. Retrieved December 5, 2022, from https://www.thespruce.com/diy-trellises-for-your-garden-1104036

*Growing Pumpkins - Pumpkins and More - University of Illinois Extension*. (n.d.). Web.extension.illinois.edu. https://web.extension.illinois.edu/pumpkins/growing.cfm

*How to Plant, Grow and Harvest Cucumbers.* (n.d.). GardenTech.com. https://www.gardentech.com/blog/garden-and-lawn-protection/ a-taste-of-summer-growing-cucumbers

*Squash (Summer) Grow Guide.* (n.d.). GrowVeg. https://www.growveg. com/plants/us-and-canada/how-to-grow-summer-squash/

Lamp'l, J. (2021, August 5). *How Do I Grow Winter Squash? | Planting & Care Guide | joegardener®.* Joe Gardener® | Organic Gardening like a Pro. https://joegardener.com/how-grow-winter-squash/

*Zucchini.* (n.d.). Almanac.com. https://www.almanac.com/plant/ zucchini

Rose, S. (2020, February 24). *Natural Pest Control - How To Plant Mixed Herbs and Vegetables To Deter Pests.* Garden Therapy. https://garden therapy.ca/deter-pests-naturally/

*7 Healthy Herbs You Should Be Cooking With.* (n.d.). EverydayHealth.com. Retrieved December 5, 2022, from https://www.everydayhealth. com/diet-nutrition-pictures/healthy-herbs-and-how-to-use-them.aspx

Lambton, C. (2014). *Growing Basil Plants: How to Plant, Care for & Harvest Basil | Fiskars.* Fiskars.com. https://www.fiskars.com/en-us/ gardening-and-yard-care/ideas-and-how-tos/planting-and-prep/ growing-basil-planting-and-harvesting

*Chive Seed Propagation - How To Grow Chives From Seed.* (n.d.). Gardening Know How. Retrieved December 5, 2022, from https:// www.gardeningknowhow.com/edible/herbs/chives/growing-chives-from-seed.htm

*Dill - How do you grow did in a garden or in containers?* (n.d.). Texas A&M AgriLife Extension Service. https://agrilifeextension.tamu.edu/ library/gardening/dill/

*Learn About Marjoram - Burpee.* (n.d.). Www.burpee.com. Retrieved December 5, 2022, from https://www.burpee.com/blog/encyclope dia__marjoram-article.html

*How to Grow Mint.* (n.d.). West Coast Seeds. https://www.westcoast seeds.com/blogs/how-to-grow/grow-mint

*How to Plant and Grow Oregano | Gardener's Path.* (2020, March 7). Gardener's Path. https://gardenerspath.com/plants/herbs/grow-oregano/

Almanac, O. F. (n.d.). *Cilantro (Coriander)*. Old Farmer's Almanac. https://www.almanac.com/plant/coriander-and-cilantro

*StackPath*. (n.d.). Www.gardeningknowhow.com. https://www.garden ingknowhow.com/edible/herbs/thyme/tips-for-growing-thyme-in-your-garden.htm

Dian. (2022, October 26). *Flowers You Should Be Growing In Your Vegetable Garden*. Dian Farmer Learning to Grow Our Own Food. https://dianfarmer.com/flowers-you-should-be-growing-in-your-vegetable-garden/

Hagen, L. (2019). *Growing Marigolds – Planting & Caring for Marigold Flowers - Garden Design*. GardenDesign.com. https://www.gardende sign.com/flowers/marigold.html

*How to Grow Nasturtiums from Seed | Gardener's Supply*. (n.d.). Www.gardeners.com. https://www.gardeners.com/how-to/grow ing-nasturtiums/7991.html

*How to Grow Calendula*. (n.d.). Www.americanmeadows.com. https://www.americanmeadows.com/wildflower-seeds/wildflower-species/how-to-grow-calendula

*How to Grow Fragrant Lavender*. (n.d.). The Spruce. https://www.thes pruce.com/growing-lavender-1402779

Vinje, E. (2022, July 14). *Complete Guide to Plant, Grow and Care for Lupine Flowers*. Planet Natural. https://www.planetnatural.com/growing-lupine/

*How to Grow Cosmos*. (2014). Americanmeadows.com. https://www.americanmeadows.com/wildflower-seeds/cosmos-flower-seeds/how-to-grow-cosmos

*The Garden Decoder: What Is "Companion Planting"?* (2021, May 13). Gardenista. https://www.gardenista.com/posts/garden-decoder-what-is-companion-planting-gardening-best-vegetable-companions/

*Companion Planting Guide for Vegetables*. (2022, May 26). Almanac.com. https://www.almanac.com/companion-planting-guide-vegetables

*StackPath*. (n.d.). Www.gardeningknowhow.com. https://www.garden ingknowhow.com/edible/herbs/hgen/companion-planting-in-your-herb-garden.htm

Gardens, W. C. (n.d.). *Companion Planting With Herbs - Garden Tips.* West Coast Gardens. Retrieved December 5, 2022, from https://westcoastgardens.ca/our-resources/companion-planting-herbs

Elizabeth. (2021, February 18). *9 Flowers You Should Plant in Your Vegetable Garden.* The Lavender Homefront. https://www.lavenderhomefront.com/companion-planting-flowers-with-vegetables/

*Transplant shock - what triggers it and how to protect plants against die-off.* (2020, May 21). Nature and Garden. https://www.nature-and-garden.com/gardening/transplant-shock.html

*10 Ways To Minimize Transplant Shock.* (2018, October 5). GardeningCalendar.ca. https://gardeningcalendar.ca/articles/transplant-shock-10-ways-to-minimize-transplanting-shock/

*Hardening Off Seedlings to Prevent Transplant Shock.* (2019, March 5). Homestead and Chill. https://homesteadandchill.com/hardening-off-seedlings/

*StackPath.* (n.d.). Www.gardeningknowhow.com. https://www.gardeningknowhow.com/garden-how-to/tools/sterilizing-pruning-tools.htm

*Saving Your Soils With Crop Rotation.* (n.d.). PartSelect.com. https://www.fix.com/blog/three-year-garden-crop-rotation-plan/

*Tilling vs. Not Tilling Gardens.* (n.d.). Home Guides | SF Gate. https://homeguides.sfgate.com/tilling-vs-not-tilling-gardens-76319.html

*What is mulching and how to mulch.* (n.d.). Gardens Illustrated. Retrieved December 5, 2022, from https://www.gardensillustrated.com/garden-advice/how-to/what-is-mulching-mulch/

*Seed Stratification Explained | Prairie Nursery.* (n.d.). Www.prairienursery.com. https://www.prairienursery.com/resources-guides/seed-stratification/

*Storing and Preserving Your Garden Harvest.* (n.d.). GrowVeg. https://www.growveg.com/guides/storing-and-preserving-your-garden-harvest/

Made in the USA
Middletown, DE
07 October 2023

40397303R00126